Bhai Ghanaiya Ji

The Embodiment of Selfless Service

Ishwar Singh

pencil

ISBN 978-93-5667-968-9
© Ishwar Singh 2023

Published in India 2023 by Pencil

A brand of
One Point Six Technologies Pvt. Ltd.
Unit no. 26, Ground Floor, Building A1,
Wadala Truck Terminal Road,
Near Post Office, Antop Hill, Mumbai - 400037
E connect@thepencilapp.com
W www.thepencilapp.com

Author biography

Ishwar Singh is a well-known and an internationally established author, whose books have been published more than 150 countries around the globe including USA, UK and Australia. He is an engineer, teacher, and public speaker. The author, a mechanical engineer by profession, has read and written poems, fiction, and research books for the past ten years. Additionally, the author is really interested in penning scholarly works on political and cultural science. Since he was 10 years old throughout his formative years, he has been a writer.

CONTENTS

Epigraph

"Love has no limitations, compassion has no restrictions, and unselfish service has no prejudice. These qualities are embodied in Bhai Ghanaiya Ji's life, and he serves as a beacon for humanity's potential for love and generosity.

Foreword

I am honored and humbled to contribute the introduction to this amazing book, "Bhai Ghanaiya Ji: The Embodiment of Selfless Service." This book explores the life and legacy of Bhai Ghanaiya Ji, a famous person in Sikh history whose deep dedication to seva (selfless service) continues to serve as an example for future generations.

The life of Bhai Ghanaiya Ji offers as a potent reminder of the transformational potential of selfless devotion and compassion in today's fast-paced society when self-centeredness and selfish ambitions often take priority. His constant commitment to helping everyone, regardless of caste, creed, or social standing, embodies the finest principles of Sikhism and represents values that are timeless and unconstrained.

Readers will go on an exploration of Bhai Ghanaiya Ji's sociocultural environment via the pages of this book, gaining insightful knowledge about the struggles, ambitions, and aspirations of the community in which he lived. The book provides a thorough narrative of his spiritual path and the influence of his connections with Guru Gobind Singh Ji, from his modest origins through his experiences with the Sikh Gurus.

The book explores Bhai Ghanaiya Ji's conception and actualization of selfless service, demonstrating how his altruistic deeds were motivated by a deep feeling of love and empathy. The anecdotes and tales that highlight his extraordinary healing abilities—not just in treating to physical wounds but also in providing peace and comfort to people in need—will enthrall readers.

This book also discusses the difficulties Bhai Ghanaiya Ji had as a result of conventional beliefs and biases, as well as how his unflinching dedication and fortitude enabled him to meet resistance head-on and carry out his great goal of helping mankind. It draws attention to his role in bridging social gaps and advancing equality, as well as his deep empathy for everyone, irrespective of caste, creed, or socioeconomic class.

Readers will have a comprehensive grasp of the importance of Bhai Ghanaiya Ji's ideals in the contemporary world as they go further into the chapters. The book looks at his seva's enduring impact and how his example continues to motivate people and organizations throughout the globe. It also looks at how his life and seva are portrayed in Sikh texts as well as how his compassion and selflessness have been expressed through art.

The book also highlights the celebrations, rituals, and occasions held to recognize Bhai Ghanaiya Ji's efforts. It underlines the customs' cultural relevance and how they serve as a constant reminder of his teachings and the value of selfless service in Sikhism.

It's significant because this book is more than just a historical overview; it issues a call to action. It motivates readers to practice unselfish service and have a good impact on their neighborhoods. It inspires people to live out the virtues of love, compassion, and service and to be conscious of the significant effects their actions may have on other people.

I applaud the author for doing in-depth study and presenting Bhai Ghanaiya Ji's life and teachings in such a thorough and interesting way. This book is a witness to the author's profound respect for Sikh history and her genuine commitment to preserving and disseminating the life stories of remarkable people.

The documentary "Bhai Ghanaiya Ji: The Embodiment of Selfless Service" is an engrossing and illuminating look at a unique person whose life continues to shed light on the importance of service and compassion for people all around the globe. I'm sure that reading this book will inspire readers, lead them on a path of self-discovery, and inspire them to believe in the transformational power of selfless service.

Amarjit Kaur

Preface

The life and teachings of Bhai Ghanaiya Ji serve as a lighthouse, lighting a path of compassion, love, and selfless service in a society that is often marked by self-interest and conflict. His extraordinary journey and steadfast dedication to humanity have forever changed Sikh history and continue to serve as an example to innumerable people all across the world.

This sincere hagiography of this beloved man in Sikh history, "Bhai Ghanaiya Ji: The Embodiment of Selfless Service," is presented in the book. In order to provide readers a better appreciation of his significant influence on the world and his eternal legacy, it seeks to bring his life, his amazing deeds of seva, and his timeless teachings to the fore.

Readers will experience a transformation as they go through the book's pages, learning about the sociocultural setting of Bhai Ghanaiya Ji's period, the factors that created his personality, and the key contacts he had with the Sikh Gurus. The book reveals Guru Gobind Singh Ji's crucial contribution to Bhai Ghanaiya Ji's spiritual development and the significant effects it had on his life.

Readers will see as the story progresses how exceptional Bhai Ghanaiya Ji's compassion and healing skills were. His steadfast adherence to the values of equality and service is shown by his unflinching commitment to caring for the injured during fights, no matter their allegiance. The book also emphasizes his attempts to overcome social barriers and subvert accepted beliefs and biases, highlighting the fact that his compassion and love are really global.

Additionally, this book includes a lot of experiences and tales that demonstrate Bhai Ghanaiya Ji's healing powers and the deep effect his deeds of compassion had on everyone who came into contact with him. His selflessness is shown by these tales, which serve as a reminder of the transformational power of love, empathy, and compassion in the context of healthcare and beyond.

The book dives deeply into the meaning of seva, the idea of selfless service at the core of Sikh teachings, in each chapter. It examines the importance of seva and its applicability to resolving social issues, promoting peace, and developing a culture of service. Readers may follow Bhai Ghanaiya Ji's knowledge and practice of selfless service as a model for adopting seva as a way of life.

This book also discusses the difficulties Bhai Ghanaiya Ji had as a result of the biases and conventional beliefs that were present at the period. It illustrates his tenacity and steadfast dedication to his beliefs, encouraging readers to endure in the face of difficulty and maintain their commitment to acts of kindness and service.

It is clear from reading this book's pages how much Bhai Ghanaiya Ji's service to the Sikh community has impacted it. His acts of kindness not only affected the lives of people, but they also served as an inspiration for organizations and institutions committed to continuing his legacy of compassion and love.

The book also examines how Bhai Ghanaiya Ji's life and service are portrayed in Sikh texts, demonstrating the esteem with which they are held there. It also looks at the numerous creative mediums that have portrayed his compassion and generosity over the ages, ensuring that his tale endures and is honored in a variety of artistic ways.

The book also describes the celebrations and activities held to recognize Bhai Ghanaiya Ji's achievements. It highlights the value of maintaining his memory via group celebrations and remembrances by revealing the festive customs and their cultural relevance.

The book "Bhai Ghanaiya Ji: The Embodiment of Selfless Service" ends with a call to action for readers to live by the principles of selfless service. It encourages readers to make a difference in their communities and contribute to the welfare of others by offering helpful advice on how to use the teachings learned from Bhai Ghanaiya Ji's seva in today's reality.

Readers of this book will be moved to consider Bhai Ghanaiya Ji's life and lasting legacy while also realizing the significant influence that acts of love, compassion, and service can have on the world. It serves as a reminder that each act of kindness has the potential to make the world a better place.

May each reader's journey through these pages inspire the spirit of service, ignite the fire of compassion, and motivate them to make a commitment to changing the world for the better. Let's continue Bhai Ghanaiya Ji's ageless message by modeling love, compassion, and selfless devotion in our own lives and in our neighborhoods.

Ishwar Singh

Acknowledgements

I want to sincerely thank and appreciate my beloved brother Hardeep Singh, whose constant support and inspiration made it possible for me to finish writing this book, "Bhai Ghanaiya Ji: The Embodiment of Selfless Service."

Hardeep has been a consistent source of inspiration and direction for me during this journey. The substance of this book has been enhanced by his extensive understanding of Sikh history, culture, and spirituality, assuring its veracity and authenticity. His priceless advice and insightful exchanges have been helpful in shaping the story and conveying the spirit of Bhai Ghanaiya Ji's life and teachings.

Hardeep's persistent commitment to the Sikh religion and his profound comprehension of the tenets of seva (selfless service) have served as a compass and reminder to me of the importance of this endeavor. His excitement for imparting the wisdom of Sikh saints and luminaries has been infectious, igniting my own desire to learn more about Bhai Ghanaiya Ji's life.

I also like to thank Hardeep for his hard research, kind criticism, and rigorous editing. The quality of this work has been much improved by his meticulous attention to detail and dedication to upholding the integrity of the text. His unflinching support has been a continual source of inspiration, even through the most trying times of this writing process.

In addition, I want to recognize Hardeep's unshakable faith in the power of storytelling and its capacity to uplift and change people. This project has been motivated by his enthusiasm for preserving and disseminating the rich history and teachings of Sikhism. His commitment to sustaining the ideals of love, kindness, and service, as shown by Bhai Ghanaiya Ji, has been an inspiration to all of us.

Finally, I want to thank Hardeep for being a friend and confidant in addition to being a brother. Throughout this writing process, his consistent encouragement, excitement, and faith in my talents have served as a continual source of inspiration. His support, affection, and helpful criticism have inspired me to work hard and produce a book that honors Bhai Ghanaiya Ji's extraordinary life and legacy.

Finally, I'd want to express my sincere appreciation to my brother Hardeep Singh for his unfailing assistance, knowledge, and commitment to this endeavor. This book would not exist if it weren't for his efforts. I am really thankful to have him as my brother because of his unfathomable impact and presence in my life.

Hardeep, I appreciate your unflinching faith in me and your business on this amazing trip. This book is a monument to our common dedication to maintaining and upholding Bhai Ghanaiya Ji's legacy and disseminating his message of love, compassion, and selfless devotion.

With sincere appreciation,

Ishwar Singh

Bhai Ghanaiya Ji

Introduction

Setting the stage: Sikhism and its emphasis on selfless service (seva)

The dynamic and open-minded religion of Sikhism was born on the Indian subcontinent in the 15th century. Sikhism, which was established by Guru Nanak Dev Ji, developed as a religion that placed a strong emphasis on spiritual awakening, equality, and selfless service. The idea of seva, which may be interpreted as selfless service performed without expecting payment or acclaim, is at the core of Sikhism. Seva is firmly anchored in the teachings of the Sikh Gurus and is seen as an essential component of the Sikh way of life.

Examining the tenets and ideas that guide Sikhism can help you understand the importance of seva in this religion. Sikhism promotes the idea that there is a single, ageless, formless heavenly being known as Ik Onkar or Waheguru. Waheguru is seen by Sikhs as the ultimate truth, and they strive to develop a close relationship with God via prayer, meditation, and moral behavior. The Sikhi way of life encourages people to participate fully in society, to help those in need, and to seek to advance mankind.

The Sikhism was founded by the enlightened spiritual figures known as the Sikh Gurus, who came after Guru Nanak Dev Ji and gave instructions on how to live a meaningful life. They were living examples of the virtues of seva, compassion, and equality via their teachings and deeds. The Gurus promoted social justice and fairness as well as the advancement of the downtrodden and the removal of societal divides. Their teachings highlighted the value of selfless service as a way to experience spiritual development and communion with the divine.

Sikhism's founder, Guru Nanak Dev Ji, established the standard for seva via his own deeds. He was a firm believer in carrying out good deeds and acts of charity that would help others and advance societal progress. In order to propagate his message of love, equality, and service, Guru Nanak Dev Ji traveled everywhere. He urged his disciples to do seva in order to purify themselves and reach spiritual enlightenment. According to Guru Nanak Dev Ji's teachings, seva includes acts of compassion, empathy, and support for others in all facets of life and is not only restricted to providing monetary aid.

Guru Angad Dev Ji, the second Guru, reaffirmed the value of seva as the lineage of Sikh Gurus went on. He started a langar, a free communal kitchen, where everyone may come together and have a meal, regardless of their socioeconomic or religious background. The institution of langar was a prime example of the values of inclusion, equality, and the abolition of social divisions. The Sikh faith's focus on serving others (seva) as a fundamental aspect of Sikhism was established by Guru Angad Dev Ji.

The idea of seva was developed and established within the Sikh community by the third Guru, Guru Amar Das Ji. Sikh congregations were divided into 22 administrative units known as manjis by Guru Amar Das Ji, who also appointed devoted people known as "manji holders" to manage the spiritual and communal well-being of the Sikh congregations. These manji bearers were in charge of encouraging people to actively participate in selfless service, promoting seva within their specific territories, and seeing to it that the requirements of the neighborhood were addressed.

The fourth Guru, Guru Ram Das Ji, kept emphasizing the value of seva. He built Amritsar, which eventually developed into the spiritual and cultural center of Sikhism. The Harmandir Sahib, sometimes referred to as the Golden Temple, was built to further stress the virtue of service. To help build this holy site, Guru Ram Das Ji urged individuals from all areas of life to donate their time, effort, and resources. The Golden Temple was built with the ideal of selfless service entrenched in its very fabric, and it still stands today as proof of the Sikh people's dedication to seva.

By writing the Adi Granth, the ancient text of Sikhism, the fifth Guru, Guru Arjan Dev Ji, enlarged the idea of service. The Adi Granth included songs written by the Sikh Gurus as well as writings from a number of saints and followers of many religions. Guru Arjan Dev Ji highlighted that seva might go beyond the physical world and encompass things like propagating the guru's teachings, safeguarding the holy texts, and encouraging peace amongst various cultures. This collection of heavenly knowledge reaffirmed the idea that doing service is a crucial component of Sikh spirituality.

The sixth Guru, Guru Hargobind Sahib Ji, further embodied seva by endorsing the warrior-saint philosophy. He taught martial skills to his disciples and stressed the value of defending oneself and the downtrodden. With his method, Guru Hargobind Sahib Ji showed that seva may take many different forms, from acts of kindness and generosity to protecting the law and resisting oppression. This comprehensive view of seva inspired Sikhs to actively carry out their duties as both spiritual beings and valuable contributors to society.

The seventh Guru, Guru Har Rai Ji, demonstrated the altruistic side of seva via his commitment to others' health and welfare. For the sake of the community, he created gardens filled with therapeutic plants and promoted the use of herbal cures. The focus of Guru Har Rai Ji on curing and caring for the ill brought home the interdependence of seva and the encouragement of mental, bodily, and spiritual welfare.

The ninth Guru, Guru Tegh Bahadur Ji, set a high standard for selfless service via his sacrifice. Guru Tegh Bahadur Ji gave his life in favor of religious freedom and the rights of the underprivileged, highlighting the need of speaking out for justice and protecting the rights of others. Sikhs are still motivated by his ultimate act of service to stand up for the underprivileged and defend morality and truth.

Lastly, the significance of seva within Sikhism was reaffirmed by Guru Gobind Singh Ji, the tenth and last human Guru. He established the Khalsa, a group of initiated Sikhs, and gave them the responsibility of upholding the values of service, bravery, and justice. Guru Gobind Singh Ji highlighted that seva extended to the wellbeing of all mankind and was not restricted to the confines of the Sikh community. He saw Sikhs as saint-soldiers and warriors who would uphold the ideal of selfless service and combat injustice and tyranny.

The Sikh Gurus laid a solid basis for seva within Sikhism via their teachings and practices. Sikhs have shown the values of seva throughout history in a variety of ways, whether it be via langar, giving refuge, offering medical care, or offering humanitarian relief during times of crisis. Sikhs are still encouraged to actively participate in acts of seva and make contributions to the betterment of society by the values of equality, compassion, and selflessness that continue to guide them in everyday life.

Seva, which has its roots in the teachings of the Sikh Gurus, is a concept that is highly valued in Sikhism. Selfless service is seen as a way to achieve spiritual fulfillment and connect with the divine by adherents of the Sikh religion. The activities of the Sikh community and the examples given forth by the Gurus reveal the transformational potential of seva and its capacity to promote compassion, equality, and social justice. Sikhs want to embody the teachings of Guru Nanak Dev Ji and the succeeding Gurus through doing service in order to make the world more inclusive and peaceful.

Introducing Bhai Ghanaiya Ji as a revered figure in Sikh history

Bhai Ghanaiya Ji stands out in the illustrious fabric of Sikh history as a renowned man whose selfless dedication and compassion have inspired generations of Sikhs. Bhai Ghanaiya Ji's life is a shining example of the fundamental Sikhism teachings, especially the idea of seva (selfless service) and the attitude of equality and all-embracing love. Bhai Ghanaiya Ji, a devout follower of Guru Gobind Singh Ji, made an imprint on Sikh history with his deeds and unflinching dedication to mankind.

Bhai Ghanaiya Ji, who was born in the latter half of the 17th century in the Punjabi hamlet of Sodhara in the modern-day Amritsar district, was brought up in a devoted Sikh household. He was influenced by the Sikh Gurus' teachings from an early age and was pulled to the path of service. His inherent compassion and steadfast adherence to the Sikhism's tenets provided the foundation for a life devoted to helping others.

The path of Bhai Ghanaiya Ji as a selfless healer started during the reign of Guru Gobind Singh Ji, the tenth Guru. Bhai Ghanaiya Ji developed as a pillar of kindness and consolation during the turbulent time of the Guru, when the Sikh community experienced severe difficulties and disputes. No matter their allegiance or creed, it is believed that he would bring a mashk (a leather water bag) filled with fresh water into the battlefield to care to the injured warriors.

During the Battle of Anandpur Sahib in 1704, one of the most well-known episodes that most exemplifies Bhai Ghanaiya Ji's unshakable dedication to seva occurred. Despite the mayhem and destruction, Bhai Ghanaiya Ji bravely entered the fray to treat the injured troops, whether they were Sikhs or opponents. He would treat their wounds with great love and care, give them water, and comfort them when they were in distress. His acts cut across racial and religious lines, exemplifying the inclusive and egalitarian aspects of Sikhism.

The assistance provided by Bhai Ghanaiya Ji wasn't ignored. When Guru Gobind Singh Ji learned of his noble deeds, he called Bhai Ghanaiya Ji into his presence. The Guru appreciated the sincerity of Bhai Ghanaiya Ji's intentions and bestowed him with a heavenly vision rather than condemning him for lending support to the adversary. Guru Gobind Singh Ji praised Bhai Ghanaiya Ji for his good works, reaffirmed the value of his seva, and urged him to keep serving mankind without bias.

Beyond the battlefield, Bhai Ghanaiya Ji's compassion was unwavering. He built a modest camp next to a river, where he continued to help the ill and the poor. Bhai Ghanaiya Ji ceaselessly helped the poor by giving them food, water, and medical attention. His generosity had no boundaries. Beyond social and religious boundaries, he gave his love and support to individuals from all walks of life, not only his fellow Sikhs.

Bhai Ghanaiya Ji's method of doing service was strongly influenced by the Sikh idea of sarbat da bhala, which is translated as "well-being for all." His deeds demonstrated his conviction that service should be provided without the hope of return or praise. Every person, in the eyes of Bhai Ghanaiya Ji, was a manifestation of the divine, and he felt it was his responsibility to promote healing and put an end to suffering.

Bhai Ghanaiya Ji's service had an effect that extended well beyond his local surroundings. Numerous others, both within and outside of the Sikh community, were moved by his altruistic deeds and were motivated to follow the seva path and develop compassion. His legacy has been indelibly etched into the annals of Sikh culture, serving as a continual reminder of the value of selfless devotion and the transformational potential of compassion and empathy.

Bhai Ghanaiya Ji is now regarded as a holy man and a representation of Sikh humanitarianism. His unselfish dedication still motivates Sikhs to do acts of seva, like as operating langars (community kitchens) or founding hospitals, schools, and philanthropic institutions. His example acts as a beacon for Sikhs, reminding them of the core principles of Sikhism and their need to serve others with compassion.

Bhai Ghanaiya Ji is venerated throughout the Sikh community due to his significant contribution to Sikh history and his personification of the virtues of seva and compassion. His constant commitment to helping others, regardless of their background, is in line with the core tenets of Sikhism and stands as a model of unconditional compassion and humanity throughout time. The life of Bhai Ghanaiya Ji serves as a source of inspiration, encouraging others to follow the path of seva and try to make the world more fair and compassionate.

Chapter 1

Birth and Early Life

1.1 Background on the socio-cultural milieu during Bhai Ghanaiya Ji's time

It is crucial to examine the socio-cultural environment of Bhai Ghanaiya Ji's period in order to fully comprehend the setting in which he lived and the effects of his acts. Bhai Ghanaiya Ji lived at a time when the Indian subcontinent saw enormous historical and social changes, notably in the Punjab area. Understanding the socio-cultural setting may help us better understand the obstacles, relationships, and societal conventions that shaped Bhai Ghanaiya Ji's life and the circumstances of his selfless devotion.

In the Indian subcontinent, the late 17th century was a time of political unrest and religious strife. Power conflicts, invasions, and shifting political environments were all observed in the Punjab area, which served as the Sikhism's birthplace. While regional forces like the Sikh Misls arose and fought for control of certain regions, the Mughal Empire, which had formerly exercised its dominion, was in decline. Bhai Ghanaiya Ji lived in a volatile socio-cultural context as a result of this complicated political situation.

The syncretic culture of the Mughal Empire, which had a sizable presence in the Punjab area, combined aspects of Persian, Central Asian, and Indian traditions. The strict religious policies of the Mughal emperors, notably Emperor Aurangzeb, created conflicts with a number of religious groups, including the Sikhs. In an effort to repress their religious traditions and deny them equal rights, the Sikh community was subjected to prejudice and persecution.

Hindus, Muslims, Sikhs, as well as many sects and castes within these religious groupings, have had an impact on the social fabric of the Punjab area. The Brahminical system had a significant impact on the deeply ingrained social structures and caste distinctions. Caste and social status-based discrimination was pervasive, dividing and promoting inequality in society.

Bhai Ghanaiya Ji lived at a period when religious intolerance and disputes between many religions were prevalent. Both the Mughal rulers and certain segments of the Hindu population persecuted the Sikh community, which later established as a separate religious community. The Sikhs opposed the then-dominant religious and societal standards in favor of establishing a society based on equality, social justice, and compassion, guided by their Gurus.

Bhai Ghanaiya Ji's deeds of selfless devotion and compassion were all the more important in this socio-cultural context. His dedication to helping people without prejudice cut beyond the lines of caste, religion, and socioeconomic class. Bhai Ghanaiya Ji's deeds offered a glimpse of a society that was more inclusive and equitable and stood in sharp contrast to the pervasive social divides and religious animosities.

A reaction to the sociocultural and theological issues of the period was the development of Sikhism. The founder of Sikhism, Guru Nanak Dev Ji, aimed to heal the gaps between various religious groups and spread a message of harmony, equality, and enlightenment. These values were further emphasized by the Sikh Gurus who came after Guru Nanak Dev Ji, who pushed Sikhs to do acts of selfless devotion and confronted the social and religious injustices of the time.

The introduction of langar, a free communal kitchen where individuals from all walks of life, regardless of their socioeconomic or religious background, could assemble and share a meal, was one of the major social initiatives initiated by the Sikh Gurus. In addition to being a useful tool for addressing hunger, the langar institution represented Sikhism's egalitarian philosophy. Langar developed become a focal location for neighborhood get-togethers, promoting a feeling of fairness, togetherness, and common humanity.

The selfless devotion of Bhai Ghanaiya Ji was in line with the principles of langar and the larger Sikh ethos. His activities were inspired by the teachings of the Sikh Gurus, who highlighted the value of seva (selfless service) as a way to achieve spiritual enlightenment. Regardless of socioeconomic or religious ties, Bhai Ghanaiya Ji's dedication to mankind broke established societal standards and embodied the inclusive philosophy of Sikhism.

Numerous spiritual and reformist groups also began to arise in Bhai Ghanaiya Ji's sociocultural environment. With their focus on individual devotion and firsthand encounters with the divine, the Bhakti and Sufi traditions gained prominence and provided different routes to reaching spiritual enlightenment. The strict social structures and rituals of traditional religious activities were often questioned by these groups.

Bhai Ghanaiya Ji's acts rang true with the greater attitude of spiritual searchers who aspired to transcend the boundaries of religious differences and social standards in such a vibrant setting. His dedication to mankind exemplified the universal values of love, compassion, and equality that cut beyond socioeconomic strata and theological distinctions.

Furthermore, Bhai Ghanaiya Ji's deeds went beyond the front lines and short-term relief operations. His dedication to unselfish service carried over into his daily activities, where he attended to the ill, gave those in need food and drink, and provided comfort. His deeds proved that seva was more than just a charitable deed; it was a concept that infused every facet of his life.

Political unrest, religious strife, and social injustice all had a role in Bhai Ghanaiya Ji's life. His time's socio-cultural environment was distinguished by a complex interaction of social hierarchies, religious orthodoxy, and power relations. In this setting, Bhai Ghanaiya Ji's acts of selfless love and compassion served as a transformational force, upending societal conventions and providing a vision of a society that is more inclusive and equal. His life serves as a striking reminder of the lasting effects of seva and the capacity for people to go above societal barriers and improve the lot of mankind.

1.2 Glimpses into his childhood, family, and upbringing

It is crucial to investigate the glimmers of Bhai Ghanaiya Ji's youth, family history, and upbringing in order to comprehend his life and journey. His temperament, morals, and ultimate career of selfless service were greatly influenced by these early experiences. Although there are few specifics concerning Bhai Ghanaiya Ji's upbringing, we may learn about his formative years by looking at historical reports and the larger socio-cultural background of the period.

His hometown was in the Sikhism heartland, a region renowned for its deeply ingrained spiritual and cultural traditions. Bhai Ghanaiya Ji would have been exposed to the Sikh Gurus' teachings from an early age while growing up in this setting, giving him a solid basis for his future spiritual path.

Bhai Ghanaiya Ji belonged to the Sikh community, which had a clear sense of self and a common goal. Sikhism's founder, Guru Nanak Dev Ji, created the groundwork for this religion by highlighting the value of meditation, moral behavior, and humanitarian assistance. These concepts were further expanded by the succeeding Sikh Gurus, who shaped the Sikh community's ethos.

The history of Bhai Ghanaiya Ji's family is not well known. But it is said that he was raised in a devoted Sikh household that valued and put the Sikh Gurus' teachings into reality. Sikhism's emphasis on equality, selfless service, and the search of spiritual enlightenment would have had a significant impact on his upbringing.

The institution of the Guru was important to the Sikh community. The Gurus were revered as spiritual mentors and role models whose teachings inspired and guided their followers. The Sikh Gurus and their teachings would have been highly revered by Bhai Ghanaiya Ji's family, who would have instilled in him a feeling of dedication and respect from a young age.

At that period, children were often taught the holy songs and texts of Sikhism by Sikh families, who placed a strong emphasis on religious education. The same would have applied to Bhai Ghanaiya Ji. He would have been exposed to the divine knowledge found in the writings of the Sikh Gurus and the Guru Granth Sahib, the holy book of Sikhism.

The Sikh Gurus stressed the values of seva (selfless service), compassion, and equality in their teachings. Bhai Ghanaiya Ji would have greatly connected with the idea of seva as a way to serve mankind and connect with the divine throughout his formative years. Regardless of societal or religious divides, he would have internalized the need of behaving with compassion and love for others as well as the value of helping others.

Bhai Ghanaiya Ji's upbringing would have been influenced by the larger socio-cultural environment of the period in addition to the religious and spiritual influences inside the Sikh community. The Punjab area was a confluence of several linguistic, cultural, and religious traditions. It was distinguished by a syncretic civilization that included aspects of Persian, Central Asian, and Indian customs.

Bhai Ghanaiya Ji was exposed to many religious and cultural traditions in this sociocultural setting, which encouraged an attitude of tolerance and acceptance. His inclusive mentality, which allowed him to see the fundamental humanity in everyone, may have been influenced by his interactions with people from different backgrounds.

Caste divides and hierarchies, especially the Brahminical system, had considerable impact on the social structure of the age. Sikhism, on the other hand, fought against these social barriers and promoted social justice and equality. Bhai Ghanaiya Ji would have grown up in a setting that promoted the ideals of equality and dignity for all people and rejected caste-based prejudice.

Bhai Ghanaiya Ji's childhood and familial circumstances are not well known, but it is clear that his upbringing gave him a strong sense of spirituality, compassion, and devotion to others. These early influences shaped his character and directed his activities, laying the groundwork for his future career of selfless service.

Bhai Ghanaiya Ji's intrinsic compassion and empathy became more obvious as he aged. Later on, he would become known as a symbol of selfless service, a renowned person whose steadfast dedication to mankind would forever be remembered in Sikh history. His background and early experiences would act as a powerful moral compass, leading him towards a career committed to helping others and easing their pain.

Despite the dearth of precise information on Bhai Ghanaiya Ji's early years, family, and upbringing, the larger socio-cultural background of the period sheds important light on these crucial years. Bhai Ghanaiya Ji absorbed the teachings of the Sikh Gurus, notably the concepts of seva, compassion, and equality as a result of growing up in a devoted Sikh household in a neighborhood that placed a strong emphasis on Sikhism. His broad worldview and strong sense of empathy were further moulded by the sociocultural context of the Punjab area, which is known for its syncretic culture and different religious traditions. His incredible path as a selfless servant of mankind, whose deeds continue to inspire generations, was shaped by these early inspirations.

Chapter 2

Path to Enlightenment

2.1 Bhai Ghanaiya Ji's spiritual journey and encounters with Sikh Gurus

Heavily influencing Bhai Ghanaiya Ji's grasp of Sikhism, enhancing his devotion to seva (selfless service), and motivating his steadfast determination to helping mankind were his spiritual journey and interactions with the Sikh Gurus. He received spiritual direction, deep insights, and a fundamental grasp of the way of love, compassion, and equality as a result of his interactions with the Sikh Gurus.

Guru Tegh Bahadur Ji, the ninth Sikh Guru, was Bhai Ghanaiya Ji's first substantial interaction with a Sikh Guru. Guru Tegh Bahadur Ji was renowned for his enlightenment, bravery, and sacrifice as a martyr for religious liberty. Bhai Ghanaiya Ji would have had the chance to hear the Guru's instructions and see firsthand how kind he was, which would have had a significant influence on his own spiritual development.

Bhai Ghanaiya Ji's dedication to helping others was strengthened while under the spiritual direction of Guru Tegh Bahadur Ji. The teachings of the Guru stressed the value of seva and the need of putting others' wellbeing before one's own. The Guru's example of selfless sacrifice and his everlasting dedication to maintaining the teachings of Sikhism would have inspired Bhai Ghanaiya Ji.

When Bhai Ghanaiya Ji met Guru Gobind Singh Ji, the tenth and last Sikh Guru, his spiritual path underwent a significant change. Sikhism was shaped by the visionary leader, poet, and warrior Guru Gobind Singh Ji, who also founded the Khalsa, the group of initiated Sikhs. For Bhai Ghanaiya Ji, this meeting would prove to be a life-changing event, increasing his comprehension of Sikh ideals and preparing him for a life of service.

Guru Gobind Singh Ji would have given Bhai Ghanaiya Ji significant spiritual understanding and direction during this meeting. The Guru highlighted the value of selfless service as a way to connect with the divine and discover one's ultimate purpose. He propagated the idea that seva was more than just doing deeds of kindness; it also included serving others with love, humility, and compassion.

Bhai Ghanaiya Ji was strongly moved by the teachings of Guru Gobind Singh Ji, which strengthened his resolve to serve mankind without prejudice. Bhai Ghanaiya Ji's commitment to easing the suffering of people in need, irrespective of their socioeconomic or religious background, would have been further fuelled by the Guru's focus on the values of equality and social justice.

Bhai Ghanaiya Ji's interactions with the Sikh Gurus helped to influence both his knowledge of Sikhism and his connection with God personally. He attained a deep spiritual understanding that affected his ideas, deeds, and worldview via their teachings and direction. Through his interactions with the Sikh Gurus, Bhai Ghanaiya Ji was able to clarify his position as a servant of mankind, enhance his sense of purpose, and develop the spiritual fortitude necessary to endure in the face of obstacles.

It is significant to note that Bhai Ghanaiya Ji's interactions with the Sikh Gurus did not take place just at certain times. Through out his life, the teachings and principles passed down by the Gurus served as a compass, influencing his thinking, forming his character, and inspiring his selfless devotion.

The spiritual development of Bhai Ghanaiya Ji and his interactions with the Sikh Gurus serve as an example of the life-changing potential of divine instruction. These experiences influenced his knowledge of Sikhism, strengthened his desire to seva, and motivated him to dedicate his life to helping others. The experience of Bhai Ghanaiya Ji serves as a reminder of the depth of spirituality and capacity for change that may be discovered via contact with enlightened beings and the lessons they offer.

2.2 The transformational impact of his interactions with Guru Gobind Singh Ji

The contacts between Bhai Ghanaiya Ji and Guru Gobind Singh Ji, the tenth Sikh Guru, had a significant and transformative effect on his life. These interactions helped him better comprehend Sikhism while also molding his personality, sense of purpose, and unshakable dedication to selfless service.

The development of Sikhism was significantly influenced by the visionary leadership of Guru Gobind Singh Ji. His teachings placed a strong emphasis on the values of bravery, equality, and seeking justice. He saw a Sikh community that would resolutely oppose injustice and fight for the wellbeing of all people.

Bhai Ghanaiya Ji would have gained important spiritual knowledge, deep insights, and a stronger sense of purpose through his contacts with Guru Gobind Singh Ji. His great knowledge of the Sikh values of seva (selfless service), equality, and compassion would have come from the Guru's teachings.

Without regard to caste, religion, or social status, Guru Gobind Singh Ji highlighted the value of serving mankind. He urged Sikhs to follow the path of love, humility, and selflessness in his teachings. This struck a profound chord with Bhai Ghanaiya Ji, strengthening his resolve to allay suffering and provide selfless service to those in need.

During the Battle of Anandpur Sahib, Bhai Ghanaiya Ji and Guru Gobind Singh Ji had one of their most important encounters. Bhai Ghanaiya Ji began attending to the injured troops on both sides of the conflict as it raged, giving them water, first aid, and consolation without distinction out of compassion and a feeling of responsibility.

When Bhai Ghanaiya Ji's acts were reported to Guru Gobind Singh Ji, the Guru called him in and questioned him about giving water to the enemy troops. Bhai Ghanaiya Ji said modestly, "I see the divine light in every being and serve them with love and compassion, without separating friend from foe."

Bhai Ghanaiya Ji's persistent dedication to seva and his in-depth knowledge of Sikh ideals impressed Guru Gobind Singh Ji, who bestowed his blessing and recognised the sincerity of his intentions. The Guru acknowledged Bhai Ghanaiya Ji as embodying the love, compassion, and service to others that are core Sikh principles.

Bhai Ghanaiya Ji's path of selfless devotion was approved and reinforced by this encounter with Guru Gobind Singh Ji. It strengthened his conviction that seva transcends distinctions and embraces all people with love and compassion. The Guru's meeting with Bhai Ghanaiya Ji strengthened his resolve to serve everyone equally and without concern for reward or credit for himself.

Bhai Ghanaiya Ji's whole life was illuminated by Guru Gobind Singh Ji's teachings and blessings. They strengthened his commitment to end suffering and provide consolation to those in need and spurred his everlasting passion to seva. His encounters with the Guru made him become a shining example of selfless service, motivating numerous others to emulate him.

Bhai Ghanaiya Ji's encounters with Guru Gobind Singh Ji had an influence that went beyond his own life. It resonated throughout Sikh history, motivating many Sikhs to follow the path of seva and fight for justice. Bhai Ghanaiya Ji's deeds and profound comprehension of Sikh ideals are still loved and honored as essential components of Sikh history.

The meetings between Bhai Ghanaiya Ji and Guru Gobind Singh Ji were crucial turning points that influenced his spiritual development and his dedication to selfless service. He gained a deeper grasp of Sikh concepts through the Guru's teachings and blessings, which also strengthened his sense of mission and reaffirmed his unshakeable commitment to serve mankind without bias. The meetings Bhai Ghanaiya Ji had with the Guru serve as an example of the transformational potential of divine instruction and the significant effects it may have on a person's life and the lives of others they touch.

Chapter 3

The Essence of Seva

3.1 Exploring the Sikh concept of seva and its significance

The core of Sikhism, Seva, which is translated as "selfless service," is of utmost importance to Sikhs. It is a notion that has a strong foundation in Sikh teachings and is regarded as a crucial component of Sikh practice. Service rendered in a spirit of humility, love, and compassion without regard for profit or individual benefit is referred to as seva. The Sikh community is shaped in large part by this idea, which advocates for social justice, equality, and everyone's well-being.

At its root, seva in Sikhism symbolizes a deeper awareness of spirituality and the interconnection of all creatures rather than just being about doing humanitarian deeds or being philanthropic. It is seen as a way to commune with the divine and live in accordance with the Sikh Gurus' teachings. Seva is seen as an act of worship, a manifestation of devotion, and a means of spiritual development.

The Sikh Gurus highlighted the value of seva in living a meaningful and purposeful life via their own actions and teachings. Sikhism's founder, Guru Nanak Dev Ji, established seva as a cornerstone of Sikh practice. He opposed asceticism and stressed the need of being actively involved in society while keeping a selfless and service-oriented mindset.

The interdependence of all creatures and the need of recognizing the holy light inside each person were both highlighted in Guru Nanak Dev Ji's teachings. He exhorted Sikhs to serve mankind without bias by putting aside differences in caste, religion, or socioeconomic class. Sikhism grew to be known for its comprehensive perspective on service, which is now upheld by Sikh communities all over the globe.

The idea of seva embraces a variety of behaviors that improve the wellbeing of others and goes beyond formal acts of service. Volunteering in communal kitchens (langars), where everyone receives free meals regardless of background or position, is one example of this. It may include helping the ill, the old, or other people of society who are marginalized, as well as taking part in environmental conservation initiatives. Seva may also be shown in daily encounters by showing compassion, generosity, and a commitment to social justice.

The institution of langar is one of Sikhism's most distinguishing examples of seva. By providing free meals to everyone who enters a Gurdwara (a Sikh house of worship), regardless of their social, economic, or religious background, Langar serves as an example of equality and community. The langar is a potent representation of dismantling boundaries, encouraging togetherness, and advancing the idea of common humanity.

Sarbat da bhala, or "welfare of all," is a practice that emphasizes the importance of seva even more. Since they understand that genuine happiness and contentment come from helping others, Sikhs want to work for the welfare of all living things. Sikhs follow this philosophy while interacting with others, which promotes kindness, compassion, and selflessness in all facets of life.

Seva has the power to drastically change lives, both for those who receive it and for those who do it. It develops appreciation, humility, and a feeling of purpose. Sikhs strive to transcend their own ego, self-centeredness, and material attachments via seva, understanding that the fundamental purpose of life is to serve others and promote social harmony.

Additionally, the Sikh community as a whole is significantly impacted by Seva. It fosters a culture of kindness, compassion, and social responsibility by establishing a feeling of solidarity. Seva promotes a culture of shared ideals and a group commitment to improving society while strengthening communal ties.

Beyond the Sikh community, the value of seva is understood and appreciated on a global scale. Humanitarian activities, disaster relief programs, and community development projects are carried out by Sikh groups and individuals, embodying the universal principles of seva and improving the lives of countless people.

Seva, or selfless service, is a fundamental Sikhism principle that exemplifies compassion, selflessness, and the quest of social justice. It is fundamentally based on the teachings of the Sikh Gurus and has a major influence on how the Sikh community is shaped. Seva is seen as a way to establish a spiritual connection, live in accordance with Sikh ideals, and promote the welfare of all living things. Sikhs want to break down barriers, advance equality, and build a society that is more compassionate and just via their acts of service, or seva. The importance of seva is found in its universal message of love, generosity, and service to mankind as well as in the transforming effects it produces on both people and communities.

3.2 Bhai Ghanaiya Ji's understanding and embodiment of selfless service

The great Sikh leader Bhai Ghanaiya Ji is known for his deep grasp and personification of selfless devotion (seva). His life and deeds are a shining example of the seva spirit, embodying the Sikhism's teachings and encouraging future generations to follow the path of compassion and selflessness.

The Sikh values of equality, humility, and love for all people were profoundly ingrained in Bhai Ghanaiya Ji's conception of seva. No matter who they were or what their circumstances, he saw the divine light inside each person. He was able to help others without regard for class, religious, or caste distinctions because to this insight.

The Battle of Anandpur Sahib served as the clearest example of Bhai Ghanaiya Ji's embodiment of selfless devotion. He gave both Sikh warriors and their adversaries drink and comfort while caring to the injured soldiers, making no distinction between friend and foe. His deeds demonstrated his faith in the universal character of seva, where the welfare of all creatures comes above all other considerations or differences of opinion.

Others were drawn to him by his conduct on the battlefield, including several Sikh troops who questioned his allegiance to the enemy. With great insight, Bhai Ghanaiya Ji replied, saying he recognized the holy light inside each individual and provided them with love and compassion. His reply demonstrated both his steadfast adherence to Sikhism's tenets and his profound comprehension of seva's all-encompassing character.

Bhai Ghanaiya Ji's conception of seva went beyond only doing deeds of service. He understood that seva included helping people in all facets of life with love, humility, and compassion. He interacted with people with understanding, compassion, and a sincere desire to lessen their pain.

Bhai Ghanaiya Ji's knowledge and practice of seva extended beyond the realm of the remarkable. He showed compassion and charity to individuals in need on a regular basis. Bhai Ghanaiya Ji accepted the chance to give others a helping hand, whether it was by giving the poor food, clothes, or shelter, attending to the ill, or comforting the bereaved.

His dedication to seva was motivated by a strong feeling of responsibility and loyalty to the teachings of the Sikh Gurus rather than by a desire for fame or personal benefit. He saw seva as a way to interact with the divine and live according to Sikhism's tenets. Bhai Ghanaiya Ji's acts demonstrated his selflessness and humility since he never sought credit or recognition for his work instead choosing to put the needs of people he helped first.

Bhai Ghanaiya Ji continues to inspire people all across the globe with his knowledge and practice of selfless service. His example serves as a potent reminder of the transforming potential of seva and its capacity to promote social justice, compassion, and togetherness. His example compels us to reflect on our own lives and choose the road of selfless service, acknowledging the inherent value and dignity in each and every person.

Finally, Bhai Ghanaiya Ji's comprehension of and practice of selfless service were profound and firmly based on Sikhism. His conduct at the Battle of Anandpur Sahib and his selfless devotion in daily life served as examples of his everlasting dedication to seva. Bhai Ghanaiya Ji's life serves as a brilliant example of the empowering potential of selflessness, motivating others to embrace seva and endeavor to build a more understanding and inclusive society.

Chapter 4

Establishing the First Aid Center

4.1 The inspiration behind Bhai Ghanaiya Ji's initiative

Bhai Ghanaiya Ji's motivation to do selfless service (seva) was motivated by his strong spiritual ties to Sikhism and his steadfast loyalty to the Sikh Gurus. His conduct was dictated by the teachings and tenets of Sikhism, which placed a high value on humanity-serving, equality, and compassion.

The life and teachings of Guru Nanak Dev Ji, the founder of Sikhism, served as an inspiration to Bhai Ghanaiya Ji. The teachings of Guru Nanak Dev Ji highlighted the unity of mankind and the need of acknowledging the divine presence within each person. These lessons were digested by Bhai Ghanaiya Ji, who then tried to make them visible via his deeds of service.

The Sikh Gurus, such as Guru Nanak Dev Ji and Guru Gobind Singh Ji, highlighted the value of selfless service as a method of establishing a spiritual connection and leading a life that has meaning. Bhai Ghanaiya Ji took these lessons to heart and realized that seva was a deep expression of love, humility, and compassion for all living things, not merely a philanthropic deed.

The idea of the langar, the communal kitchen started by Guru Nanak Dev Ji, also served as inspiration for Bhai Ghanaiya Ji's effort. People from different backgrounds are invited to enjoy a shared meal at a langar, which stands for equality, togetherness, and the removal of societal boundaries. In order to spread the inclusiveness and service-oriented ideas of langar beyond the confines of the langar hall, Bhai Ghanaiya Ji realized the transforming potential of the meal.

Bhai Ghanaiya Ji further found inspiration in the examples given out by the Sikh Gurus themselves. The Gurus were revered for their generous acts of kindness, compassion, and commitment to the well-being of others. Bhai Ghanaiya Ji saw himself as a devout follower of the Gurus, making an effort to imitate their attitude of service in his own life.

His motivation was also sparked by the misery and difficulties he saw all around him. Bhai Ghanaiya Ji was profoundly impacted by the hardship and difficulties people in society were going through, and he felt a tremendous inner need to help them out. His attempt to provide consolation, comfort, and care to individuals in need, regardless of their background or circumstances, was motivated by his empathy and compassion.

Bhai Ghanaiya Ji's idea was inspired by a sincere desire to help others and lead a meaningful life rather than by the desire for fame or personal wealth. His love for the Sikh Gurus, his connection to Sikh teachings, and his genuine compassion for other people's difficulties served as his sources of inspiration.

Bhai Ghanaiya Ji's effort to practice selfless service was motivated by his deep spiritual ties to Sikhism, his love for the Sikh Gurus, and his comprehension of the religion's teachings on equality, compassion, and service. In addition, the Gurus' own examples and his profound compassion for the suffering of others served as major sources of motivation for him. Bhai Ghanaiya Ji's endeavor to provide selfless service keeps motivating others to choose the path of kindness and service to others.

4.2 Challenges faced and the creation of a sanctuary for healing and compassion

Bhai Ghanaiya Ji had to overcome many obstacles in his quest to establish a haven of compassion and healing. Despite his admirable objectives and unshakable commitment, he ran across criticism and pushback from a number of sources. He had to overcome these obstacles and go through trying situations in order to create a place of love, healing, and compassion.

The prejudice and hostility of the general public was one of the main difficulties Bhai Ghanaiya Ji faced. It was challenging for Bhai Ghanaiya Ji to win support for his inclusive service philosophy since the inflexible societal institutions of the period often supported prejudice and division. Some others questioned his behavior, notably the attention and support he gave to those who were seen as misfits or disadvantaged by society. In order to promote the inherent value and dignity of every person, Bhai

Ghanaiya Ji had to face and combat these engrained biases and prejudices.

The lack of resources and assistance was another major problem. It took tangible means and the aid of like-minded people to create a refuge for healing and compassion. Bhai Ghanaiya Ji had to overcome the constraints of low resources and mobilize community support to maintain and grow his activities. To assure the delivery of crucial services to people in need, he had to marshal resources and depend on the kindness of others.

Bhai Ghanaiya Ji also faced hostility from individuals who disagreed with his conduct or thought they went against accepted religious or social standards. His method of providing service was questioned by those who said it ignored established boundaries or hierarchies. Bhai Ghanaiya Ji had to deal with these accusations and make a compelling argument for his inclusive and compassionate vision, grounded in Sikhism's teachings and the ideals of love and humanity that apply to all people.

Bhai Ghanaiya Ji furthermore has issues with lifespan and sustainability. A refuge for healing and compassion needed to be established, and this took time, money, and support. Bhai Ghanaiya Ji had to create the structures and mechanisms necessary to maintain his mission after his passing. This involves fostering a culture of kindness and service throughout the community by educating and enabling others to continue on the job of seva.

Despite these obstacles, Bhai Ghanaiya Ji was able to establish a haven of compassion and healing because to his persistent will and the help of like-minded people. His actions, such as giving ill and suffering people medical attention, consolation, and assistance, were well-known for their profound effects. Through his work, Bhai Ghanaiya Ji built places of love where people might find comfort, care, and the curative effects of compassion.

The shelter Bhai Ghanaiya Ji built became a symbol of hope and proof of how selfless service can change people's lives. It developed into a location where people from all walks of life could find solace, get assistance, and see the therapeutic value of compassion. The sanctuary offered a place of refuge and healing to people in need, serving as a concrete representation of the Sikh ideals of equality, love, and service.

Bhai Ghanaiya Ji encountered many difficulties in his quest to establish a haven of compassion and healing. He had to deal with social opposition, resource depletion, opposition, and sustainability issues. He was able to overcome these obstacles and create places of compassion and healing because to his unshakeable resolve, which was inspired by Sikhism. Bhai Ghanaiya Ji's initiatives continue to motivate people to establish places of compassion and service that nurture healing and further the welfare of all creatures.

Chapter 5

Healing with Love

5.1 Anecdotes and stories illustrating Bhai Ghanaiya Ji's healing abilities

Many tales and stories have been handed down through the centuries demonstrating the deep influence of Bhai Ghanaiya Ji's compassion and care. His healing talents were legendary. These tales reveal his amazing capacity for comforting, consoling, and mending the hurting. The following examples demonstrate Bhai Ghanaiya Ji's exceptional healing abilities:

- The Wounded Soldier: Bhai Ghanaiya Ji's compassion and healing skills were on full display at the Battle of Anandpur Sahib. He observed a seriously wounded soldier who had lost consciousness as he went among the stricken men. Water and comfort were lovingly administered to the soldier's wounds by Bhai Ghanaiya Ji. The soldier miraculously recovered consciousness, and his injuries quickly started to heal. This event not only showed Bhai Ghanaiya Ji's physical healing skills, but also his capacity to comfort and inspire hope in those facing overwhelming adversity.

- The Sick kid: In a separate occurrence, a woman came to Bhai Ghanaiya Ji asking for assistance on behalf of her very sick kid. All medical attempts to treat the child's crippling sickness had been unsuccessful for a protracted period of time. In his arms, Bhai Ghanaiya Ji comforted and prayed for the child's safety. To everyone's surprise, the child's health began to progressively improve. Both the mother and the kid were ecstatic with Bhai Ghanaiya Ji's kind presence and curative touch.

- Healing the Outcast: Regardless of a person's place in society, Bhai Ghanaiya Ji showed compassion to everybody. In one instance, a person who was stigmatized by society because of a communicable illness was involved. Bhai Ghanaiya Ji bravely approached the ostracized, seeing to their wounds and offering compassion despite the dangers. The outcast received both physical recovery and a feeling of dignity and belonging because to his continuous love and dedication. Bhai Ghanaiya Ji's gesture of kindness defied social conventions and served as an example of the Sikh value of inclusion and equality.

- The Blind Person's Vision: Bhai Ghanaiya Ji's healing powers extended to issues of the heart and spirit in addition to bodily illnesses. One account describes a run-in with a blind individual who asked for help. Bhai Ghanaiya Ji prayed fervently and blessed the individual physically. Thankfully, the blind person's eyesight was recovered, allowing them to once again view the outside world. This occurrence demonstrated Bhai Ghanaiya Ji's capacity to provide individuals in need inner healing, hope, and spiritual development.

- The Recuperation of the disabled Man: One day, a man who had been disabled for a long time came to Bhai Ghanaiya Ji in despair. He had tried several different therapies and cures but had no success. Bhai Ghanaiya Ji was saddened by the man's situation and put his hands on his legs while frantically praying. The guy gradually began to experience a warm feeling in his legs, and to his surprise, he was able to gather his strength and walk again. A live example of Bhai Ghanaiya Ji's medical prowess, the man's recovery was seen as a remarkable change.

- Healing the Emotional scars: Bhai Ghanaiya Ji has the capacity to treat not just physical maladies but also psychological and emotional scars. One grieving person who had just lost a loved one came to Bhai Ghanaiya Ji looking for comfort and advice. Bhai Ghanaiya Ji listened carefully while providing consoling remarks and a caring presence. The person received comfort, healing, and a newfound feeling of hope to manage their loss and go on in life via his sympathetic understanding and wise remarks.

- Restorating Mental tranquility: Bhai Ghanaiya Ji's healing touch was renowned for its capacity to relieve emotional suffering and bring about a state of mental tranquility. A person seeking relief from excruciating tension and worry went to Bhai Ghanaiya Ji. Bhai Ghanaiya Ji laid a kind hand on the individual's head and prayed for their welfare. The person's anxiousness subsided as they attained inner peace, and they felt a deep feeling of serenity and clarity. This experience proved Bhai Ghanaiya Ji's ability to provide spiritual and emotional healing.

- Healing the Wounds of Society: Bhai Ghanaiya Ji's healing powers went beyond treating specific patients and included treating the wounds of society as a whole. In times of strife and hostility, Bhai Ghanaiya Ji would make concerted efforts to bring communities together and promote unity. His empathetic presence and attempts to build bridges had a profoundly transforming effect, aiding in the healing of ruptured bonds and the scars left by social strife.The powerful effects of Bhai Ghanaiya Ji's healing talents and his embodiment of compassion are evident in these experiences and stories. His activities had a deeper impact on people's lives than just providing physical treatment. Those who sought out Bhai Ghanaiya Ji's aid found comfort, peace, and change in his presence, care, and prayers. His extraordinary healing talents became a symbol of the efficacy of kindness, love, and unselfish service.

It is important to remember that these tales are handed down orally and may have changed through time. However, they function as potent reminders of Bhai Ghanaiya Ji's exceptional healing talents and tremendous effect, encouraging future generations to follow the path of love, healing, and selfless devotion.

These anecdotes and tales provide a window into Bhai Ghanaiya Ji's incredible healing prowess. His presence and loving activities profoundly improved the lives of individuals who sought his help, whether via physical healing, emotional support, or spiritual development. These tales serve as a timely reminder of the ability of love, empathy, and selfless service to heal, inspire hope, and change people and communities.

It is essential to remember that these tales are statements of religion and belief in addition to being firmly established in Sikh culture and providing inspiration. Although everyone may interpret and perceive these incidents differently, they continue to be potent reminders of Bhai Ghanaiya Ji's legacy and his capacity to provide comfort and compassion to people who are suffering.

5.2 The power of love, empathy, and kindness in his approach to healthcare

The principles of love, empathy, and compassion were the foundation of Bhai Ghanaiya Ji's approach to treatment. His deeds embodied the fundamental values of Sikhism, highlighting the significance of selfless service (seva) and the understanding of the divine inside each and every person. Bhai Ghanaiya Ji emphasised a person's whole health in his approach to healthcare, realizing that genuine healing extended beyond the physical.

The foundation of Bhai Ghanaiya Ji's philosophy of medicine was love. He acted with sincere concern and regard for people he served because he knew that love had the capacity to heal and change. People seeking treatment were able to feel safe and at ease because to his friendly demeanor and empathetic presence. His attempts to end pain and reestablish wellbeing were motivated by love.

Another important component of Bhai Ghanaiya Ji's strategy was empathy. He aggressively tried to sympathize with their situations since he had a profound grasp of the suffering and difficulties endured by persons seeking medical attention. Bhai Ghanaiya Ji would pay close attention to people and let them express their worries, anxieties, and feelings. He was able to provide them individualized care and support that took into account all the many facets of recovery because he took the time to thoroughly understand their needs and feelings.

Bhai Ghanaiya Ji's encounters with those seeking medical treatment were based on kindness. Regardless of their history or circumstances, he showed the highest respect, decency, and compassion to everyone. Bhai Ghanaiya Ji made a special effort to make people feel important, visible, and heard because he understood the transformative power of compassion. In addition to offering physical care, he also showed compassion by offering spiritual comfort and mental support.

The way that Bhai Ghanaiya Ji approached healthcare went beyond the transactional aspect of medical care. He understood that promoting comfort, optimism, and support for people while they through recovery was just as important as treating physical ills. With patients, Bhai Ghanaiya Ji would sit and hold their hands while speaking uplifting words and imparting spiritual counsel. He thought that the force of true human connection and presence might heal and lessen pain.

His method of providing healthcare also went against prejudices and cultural standards. Without regard for socioeconomic strata or divides, Bhai Ghanaiya Ji showed compassion and equal attention to every person. He cared for those who were rejected, mistreated, or treated poorly by society. Bhai Ghanaiya Ji aimed to break down barriers and promote a more inclusive and fair approach to healthcare by showing compassion and caring to everyone.

People are still motivated by Bhai Ghanaiya Ji's method of providing treatment today. His focus on love, empathy, and compassion serves as a reminder of the significant influence that these traits can have on people's lives and the wellbeing of whole communities. His legacy serves as a potent reminder that healthcare involves more than simply treating physical illnesses; it also entails accepting each person's humanity, encouraging connection, and supporting healing on many other levels. Bhai Ghanaiya Ji showed the transformational potential of a compassionate approach to treatment by emulating love, understanding, and kindness.

Chapter 6

Serving on the Battlefield

6.1 Bhai Ghanaiya Ji's role in tending to the wounded during battles

Bhai Ghanaiya Ji demonstrated his steadfast dedication to compassion and service in the midst of difficulty by playing a vital role in caring for the injured during wars. His on-the-field deeds embodied the seva (selfless service) attitude at the core of Sikhism and had a profound effect on the lives of innumerable people.

Regardless of their membership or loyalty, Bhai Ghanaiya Ji actively participated in providing medical help and treatment to the injured throughout times of war and strife. He understood that the pain brought on by conflict had no bounds and that everyone needed compassion and healing.

Bhai Ghanaiya Ji would bravely maneuver through the turmoil and devastation on the battlefield while caring to the injured men. His efforts were driven by a profound feeling of empathy and a need to lessen their suffering. He would administer emergency first aid, bind wounds, and offer consolation and comfort to people who were in need.

Bhai Ghanaiya Ji stood out for his capacity to look across the lines dividing the battlefield. Regardless of their side or allegiance, he regarded every injured soldier as a fellow human being worthy of compassion. With a focus on our common humanity and the worth of every person, this inclusive strategy questioned traditional ideas about combat.

The teachings of the Sikh Gurus, especially Guru Nanak Dev Ji's message of equality and Guru Gobind Singh Ji's focus on selfless service, were the inspiration for Bhai Ghanaiya Ji's deeds. He displayed the Sikh philosophy of "Sarbat da Bhala," which means the welfare of everyone, by working tirelessly to care for the injured.

In the midst of the destruction of combat, his presence and his acts offered a ray of hope. Bhai Ghanaiya Ji's compassion would provide comfort to the soldiers, and they would be emotionally moved by his sacrificial devotion. In addition to treating their bodily wounds, his comforting touch, kind words, and careful attention also elevated their spirits and provided solace in their darkest hours.

The work of Bhai Ghanaiya Ji on the battlefield went beyond providing emergency medical care. He would also provide the injured warriors emotional assistance, speaking words of inspiration, and spiritual direction to boost their spirits. In the middle of the war, his presence became a source of support and inspiration for many who had lost hope.

His acts extended beyond a particular conflict or incident and established himself as a constant on the battlefield.

When someone was hurt, Bhai Ghanaiya Ji would go out of his way to find them and treat them with compassion and healing. His altruistic assistance in the midst of the turmoil of war became legendary, and his name came to represent devotion to the welfare of others.

The Sikh principles of compassion, equality, and selfless service were most illustrated by Bhai Ghanaiya Ji's care of the injured during fights. His deeds acted as a warning that empathy and compassion should triumph even in the face of battle. His legacy continues to motivate people to practice seva, acknowledge the inherent value and dignity of every person, and actively strive for the welfare of everyone.

6.2 Bravery and compassion amidst the chaos of war

Bhai Ghanaiya Ji shown great courage and compassion amid the chaos of war, when violence and devastation rule. His constant dedication to helping others—even under the most dangerous conditions—displayed the strength of his character and the breadth of his compassion.

Bhai Ghanaiya Ji's gallantry was not motivated by a desire for individual fame or military triumph. Rather, it came from his deep comprehension of the Sikh teachings, which placed a strong emphasis on altruism and the wellbeing of others. He bravely into the thick of the fighting, unfazed by the perils that surrounded him, motivated only by his commitment to easing pain and giving solace to the injured.

Despite the pandemonium of war, Bhai Ghanaiya Ji persisted in his duty to care for the injured, regardless of their loyalty or affiliation. He saw the common humanity of all those affected by war's ravages, seeing through divides and hostility. His courage resided in his capacity to cross barriers and provide kindness and compassion to both allies and adversaries.

The courage shown by Bhai Ghanaiya Ji extended beyond only providing emergency medical care. To save individuals who were imprisoned or wounded, he would travel into regions of fierce combat while putting his own safety in danger. He would shelter injured troops from danger, transport them to safety, and provide them the attention and assistance they so desperately needed. In the turmoil and misery of the battlefield, his valiant deeds served as a light of hope.

In addition to his courage, Bhai Ghanaiya Ji's compassion was evident in all of his deeds. With compassion, understanding, and a healing touch, he tried to lessen the suffering of the injured troops by acknowledging their pain, fear, and trauma. He would comfort them, support them emotionally, and let them know they weren't alone in their troubles.

The kindness of Bhai Ghanaiya Ji went beyond what the injured people needed right away. He worked to foster healing and reconciliation because he was aware of the enduring effects that conflict had on people and communities. His deeds of kindness went beyond the front lines and into the years after the war. He would actively participate in initiatives to rehabilitate neighborhoods, improve mutual understanding, and advance peace.

Bhai Ghanaiya Ji's courage and kindness stood out in the midst of the turmoil of war as a potent reminder of the Sikhism's core principles. He showed that the values of love, empathy, and selfless service could triumph even under the harshest and most difficult circumstances. His deeds motivated others to rise above the horrors of war and exhibit humanity and compassion.

Bhai Ghanaiya Ji's compassion and courage in the middle of the turmoil of war still serve as an example to people today. His legacy is proof of the transformational power of selflessness and the significant influence that acts of kindness can have, even in the most trying of circumstances. His example challenges us to consider how courageous and compassionate we can be, encouraging us to develop these traits and actively strive towards a more peaceful and caring society.

The bravery of Bhai Ghanaiya Ji extended beyond his bravery on the battlefield. He also shown great moral bravery by questioning the established rules of war. Bhai Ghanaiya Ji emerged as a light of compassion at a time when conflict was often conducted with a strong feeling of anger and contempt for the foe, breaching social norms.

His steadfast dedication to kindness and devotion in the midst of conflict demonstrated his profound faith in the inherent value and dignity of every person. Bhai Ghanaiya Ji saw the injured troops as fellow human beings instead than as foes to be vanquished. The Sikh ideals of equality and compassion for everyone served as his compass.

Bhai Ghanaiya Ji shown tremendous calmness and bravery in the midst of conflict. Despite the turmoil and danger all around him, he maintained his composure and attention. He was courageous because he had a strong sense of purpose and a clear knowledge of his duty as a peacemaker and healer in the middle of a violent conflict.

Acts of valor performed by Bhai Ghanaiya Ji were often completed under stressful circumstances. He continued on with his objective despite the noises and images of war, the screams of the injured, and the continual fear of harm. Instead, he found strength in his unshakeable faith and steadfast dedication to serving people.

His humanitarian deeds on the front lines served as a potent lesson on the transforming potential of kindness and empathy. Bhai Ghanaiya Ji used compassion as his weapon in the face of animosity and violence because he understood the need of mending hurts and promoting understanding for the establishment of permanent peace.

Bhai Ghanaiya Ji showed via his deeds that boldness and compassion are not incompatible qualities. In actuality, they may reinforce and support one another. His unshakeable fearlessness was strengthened by a deep reservoir of compassion, which inspired his courageous deeds.

Bhai Ghanaiya Ji's example still serves as motivation for people today, serving as a reminder of the enormous power of compassion and empathy to promote healing and reconciliation in the face of strife. His legacy urges us to adopt a more forgiving and inclusive attitude to conflict resolution and encourages us to resist the dominant narratives of aggressiveness and hatred.

Bhai Ghanaiya Ji's courage and compassion give a glimmer of hope in a world often characterized by division and hate. They urge us to rise above the turmoil and violence, to see beyond divisions, and to see the common humanity in each person. They encourage us to actively contribute to the creation of a more peaceful and compassionate society by developing bravery and compassion in our own lives.

The courage and kindness shown by Bhai Ghanaiya Ji in the midst of the mayhem of war have forever changed Sikh history. His example will serve as a beacon for future generations, teaching us that even under the most difficult circumstances, compassion, empathy, and selfless service can triumph and change people's lives.

Chapter 7

Upholding Equality and Social Justice

7.1 Bhai Ghanaiya Ji's efforts to bridge societal divides and promote equality

Bhai Ghanaiya Ji's objective of selfless service (seva) was centered on bridging social gaps and advancing equality, which was in line with Sikhism's basic tenets. He aggressively strived to promote harmony, understanding, and equality because he saw how social divides and disparities hampered the wellbeing of people and communities.

One of Bhai Ghanaiya Ji's major accomplishments was his capacity to cross socioeconomic divides and provide all people with the same level of compassion and care. Bhai Ghanaiya Ji served everyone with steadfast commitment at a period when caste-based prejudice and societal hierarchies were pervasive. Recognizing the inherent value of every human being, he treated everyone with the same respect, regardless of their position in life.

His activities promoted a bold vision of equality while challenging the social conventions that were in place. Bhai Ghanaiya Ji's dedication to serve everyone equally became a potent protest against societal differences and a reminder of the inherent equality at the heart of Sikh teachings.

Bhai Ghanaiya Ji aimed to bridge the gaps between various socioeconomic groups and promote a spirit of brotherhood and togetherness through his selfless service. His programs were inclusive, welcoming people from many backgrounds and establishing places where people from different socioeconomic classes and backgrounds could mingle.

Bhai Ghanaiya Ji aimed to promote equality by focusing on both the immediate needs of those in need and addressing the underlying causes of societal divides and inequality. He participated in discussions and discourse, urging people to consider their preconceptions and prejudices. According to Bhai Ghanaiya Ji, genuine equality could only be attained when everyone agreed that each person had intrinsic value and joined together to end discriminatory behaviors.

The activities of Bhai Ghanaiya Ji went beyond only providing medical assistance. He aggressively fought to provide underprivileged people and communities with resources, chances for development, and access to education. Bhai Ghanaiya Ji sought to build a more fair and equitable society by aiding and promoting individuals who had been previously mistreated or disregarded.

His support for equality and social justice was shown via his own deeds rather than simply words. Bhai Ghanaiya Ji challenged ideas of financial prosperity and social position by living a life of simplicity and humility. He stressed the value of putting others' needs above one's own, encouraging people to do the same in their own lives.

Bhai Ghanaiya Ji's efforts to promote equality and heal social rifts had a long-lasting effect on Sikh society. His legacy continues to motivate people to speak out against social injustices, remove obstacles, and make active efforts to create a society that is more inclusive and equal. His example serves as a potent reminder that real equality can only be attained when we acknowledge the divinity in each person and work for justice and fairness for all.

Bhai Ghanaiya Ji's ideal of equality and togetherness still holds true in a society when social divides and inequality persist. His example and teachings encourage us to reflect on our own prejudices, fight against prejudice, and actively advance tolerance and equality in all spheres of life. We can help create a more fair and compassionate society where everyone is treated with respect and dignity, regardless of their social background, by accepting his teachings and following in his footsteps.

7.2 His compassion towards all regardless of caste, creed, or social status

Bhai Ghanaiya Ji's unique personality was characterized by his compassion for all people, regardless of caste, creed, or social standing. He upheld the teachings of Sikh Gurus that highlighted the oneness of people and the rejection of societal hierarchies and embodied the Sikh concept of equality.

Bhai Ghanaiya Ji broke societal conventions in a culture that was firmly rooted in caste-based prejudice and social divides by treating everyone with the same amount of love, respect, and compassion. He understood that one's value or the degree of care and compassion they deserved should not be based on caste, creed, or social rank.

Bhai Ghanaiya Ji's compassion extended to everyone, not just the well-off or powerful. He aggressively sought out those who were oppressed, mistreated, or disadvantaged by society, offering his kind hand to help them. He was committed to meet their needs and lessen their suffering since he knew that individuals who were socially disadvantaged often encountered extra difficulties.

His strategy was all-inclusive, welcoming people from all backgrounds. Without distinction, he would provide services to the rich and the poor, the lofty and the low. Every person has a divine spark, according to Bhai Ghanaiya Ji, and he thought that everyone deserved to be treated with kindness, respect, and dignity. He treated everyone equally, tearing down social class boundaries and fostering a spirit of fraternity and solidarity.

Bhai Ghanaiya Ji's selfless deeds were not motivated by personal gain or any hidden agendas. He was only motivated by his intense empathy and dedication to the welfare of everyone when he selflessly helped others. He showed true, unwavering compassion to everyone he came into contact with, regardless of their social station or background.

By providing compassionate service, Bhai Ghanaiya Ji hoped to eliminate the societally-erected obstacles and promote equality and harmony. He believed that only until the inherent dignity and value of every person were acknowledged and honored could real spiritual development and social progress be attained.

Even now, Bhai Ghanaiya Ji's kindness to everyone, regardless of caste, race, or social standing, remains an inspiration. His example pushes us to consider our own preconceptions and biases, to overcome societal barriers, and to see the fundamental equality and value of every person.

His legacy encourages us to actively strive toward establishing a society in which compassion serves as the guiding ideal and where people are assessed on the quality of their character rather than their social standing. By following in his footsteps and emulating his attitude of compassion, we may help create a society that is more accepting and peaceful and in which each person is treated with respect, love, and dignity.

The fundamental Sikhism teachings, which place a strong emphasis on the unity of people and reject societal distinctions, are the source of Bhai Ghanaiya Ji's compassion. He understood that societal constructs like caste, religion, or social rank are not fundamental to the human experience. This knowledge was shown by his caring acts, which included treating everyone with the same amount of love and respect.

His contacts with individuals from different backgrounds demonstrated his sincere concern and care for their welfare. Bhai Ghanaiya Ji considered everyone as fellow humans worthy of compassion and assistance and did not distinguish between them based on their caste or social status. His deeds served as a powerful example of how Sikh teachings, which reject prejudice and promote equality, are inclusive.

The kindness of Bhai Ghanaiya Ji was not limited to members of his community or religious organization.

Recognizing the intrinsic value and dignity of every human being, he extended his care and support to people of other religions and origins. His gestures of kindness cut across religious lines and promoted harmony and understanding across many faiths.

His empathy for everyone, regardless of caste, religion, or social standing, defied the societal mores that prevailed at the time. It was a ground-breaking strategy meant to destroy the inherent social divides and hierarchies. The deeds of Bhai Ghanaiya Ji served as a potent reminder that real spirituality consists in accepting the shared humanity that binds us all.

His compassion extended beyond surface-level exchanges and reached far into the lives and emotions of individuals he came into contact with. He sincerely understood the challenges and tribulations that others experienced, and his kind deeds were often accompanied by words of consolation, inspiration, and direction. Those who felt excluded or forgotten by society found solace and confidence in Bhai Ghanaiya Ji's loving presence.

Even in the face of resistance or criticism, he remained steadfast in his devotion to compassion. No of their socioeconomic status, Bhai Ghanaiya Ji firmly believed that everyone was deserving of respect, love, and care. His acts compelled others to examine their own preconceptions and biases, which led them to adopt a more accepting and kind attitude toward others.

Bhai Ghanaiya Ji's kindness to everyone serves as a beacon of hope for future generations. His example continues to encourage others to shed the constraints of cultural divides and to adopt a more accepting and egalitarian way of thinking. His legacy pushes us to consider our own beliefs and actions, encouraging us to develop compassion and treat everyone we come into contact with with love, respect, and decency.

Bhai Ghanaiya Ji's compassion for all people, irrespective of caste, race, or social class, serves as a timeless reminder of the transformational power of love and empathy in a society that still struggles with prejudice and societal divides. His example encourages us to overcome our differences and strive towards a more compassionate and just society where everyone is treated equally, fairly, and with compassion.

Chapter 8

Challenges and Opposition

8.1 Opposition faced by Bhai Ghanaiya Ji due to traditional norms and prejudices

Bhai Ghanaiya Ji has faced resistance and criticism because of his selfless deeds and contempt for social conventions and biases. The deeply rooted social hierarchies and biases of his period were challenged by his philosophy of treating every person with the same care and respect.

People who were firmly rooted in the established social order, which was founded on caste, faith, and social standing, were one of the main sources of resistance. These distinctions were ignored by Bhai Ghanaiya Ji's compassionate service, which accorded everyone the same amount of love and attention. This jeopardized the privileged positions of those who profited from the current system and posed a challenge to the established power relations. They opposed Bhai Ghanaiya Ji's inclusive style because they saw his acts as a threat to their own social standing.

Individuals with deep-seated prejudices and biases against certain castes or social groupings also opposed the movement. Bhai Ghanaiya Ji was seen as directly challenging these stereotypes by refusing to discriminate on the basis of caste or social standing. certain people were unable to understand him and chastised him for defying societal conventions that mandated the superiority of certain groups over others because they were so limited in their thinking.

Additionally, Bhai Ghanaiya Ji's compassionate attitude was not easily accepted by the time's religious orthodoxy. His acts were seen as being out of the ordinary and in opposition to the strict religious rites and rituals that were prioritized. He valued giving and compassion more than customary religious rites, which went against the existing ecclesiastical hierarchy. People who were hesitant to accept an alternative interpretation of religious teachings reacted negatively to this.

Bhai Ghanaiya Ji encountered resistance that went beyond verbal rebuke and social marginalization. He sometimes encountered unpleasant people who directly threatened him or threatened to attack him physically because of his inclusive attitude. Some people used violent tactics to stifle his message of equality and compassion because they saw his activities as a threat to their own authority or social position.

Bhai Ghanaiya Ji persisted in his dedication to his values in the face of resistance. Despite the obstacles, he persisted in serving others selflessly and shown everlasting compassion for everyone. Others found inspiration in his tenacity and unshakable commitment to his cause, which strengthened their faith in the transforming power of compassion and upended the status quo.

Bhai Ghanaiya Ji's deeds and teachings were eventually acknowledged and accepted both inside and beyond the Sikh community. Many people were moved by his message of equality and compassion, and his legacy continues to motivate others to confront stereotypes, knock down barriers, and fight for a more compassionate and inclusive society.

Bhai Ghanaiya Ji received pushback because of prejudice and conventional standards, which underscores the difficulties faced by people who work to promote equality and question social conventions. His story serves as a reminder of the value of tenacity and fortitude in the face of challenges, as well as the transforming effects that may be attained by confronting deeply rooted biases and preconceptions.

Bhai Ghanaiya Ji encountered criticism because of a number of social, cultural, and religious elements that were embedded in the culture of his day. Social interactions were governed by outdated rules and preconceived notions, which reinforced divides based on caste, faith, and social standing. Bhai Ghanaiya Ji was criticized and opposed because his altruistic deeds immediately transgressed these standards.

People were given certain tasks and obligations under the rigorous caste system that predominated throughout society depending on their birth. It was against the established order for Bhai Ghanaiya Ji to serve everyone regardless of caste and to overlook caste differences.

People who considered lower caste members to be socially inferior and regarded their own caste to be superior found this upsetting. They were opposed because they were concerned about losing their social rank and sense of superiority.

Bhai Ghanaiya Ji encountered criticism due to prejudices based on religious differences as well. Tensions often developed between various religious groups in a society that was characterized by religious variety. Bhai Ghanaiya Ji questioned the idea of religious exclusivity by taking an inclusive stance and showing compassion to people of all religions. His message of love and compassion was universal, but some people struggled to embrace it because of religious preconceptions, which sparked criticism.

Individuals were not the only ones opposed; organized religious organizations and the time's orthodox religious leaders were also opposed. The hierarchical structure of religious authority was in danger as a result of Bhai Ghanaiya Ji's focus on the essential values of compassion and service. His activities avoided formal religious rites and customs and put more emphasis on the spiritual and personal aspects of life. As a result, many in positions of authority and influence inside religious organizations rebelled against the established religious order.

Bhai Ghanaiya Ji persisted in his dedication to his values in the face of resistance. He thought that the core Sikh teachings should transcend societal barriers and center on compassion and service. Others were motivated to examine their own biases and prejudices by his tenacity in the face of criticism and opposition. His message of equality and compassion acquired more traction throughout time, and his deeds served as an example for succeeding generations.

Bhai Ghanaiya Ji's perseverance in the face of criticism to his purpose revealed his everlasting faith in the potential of love and empathy to bridge social gaps. His activities had a lasting impression on the Sikh community and other communities by challenging the entrenched biases and social structures of his period. His example continues to encourage others to question conventional beliefs and biases, advancing inclusion and equality in all facets of life.

Bhai Ghanaiya Ji's resistance serves as a reminder of the challenges faced by individuals who work to overcome social restrictions and advance a more compassionate and inclusive society. It emphasizes the need for people to actively strive towards eradicating biases and advancing unity and equality while being steadfast in their views in the face of difficulty. Bhai Ghanaiya Ji's legacy serves as a reminder of the significance of standing up for what is right in the face of criticism and the transformational power of compassion.

8.2 His steadfast commitment and resilience in the face of adversity

Bhai Ghanaiya Ji's unwavering dedication and fortitude in the face of difficulty were exceptional traits that characterized him and his purpose. He faced resistance, criticism, and even violent threats, yet he never wavered in his commitment to lovingly and compassionately serve mankind.

His dedication was a result of his strong trust in Sikhism's tenets. Bhai Ghanaiya Ji saw that genuine spirituality transcended ceremonies and outward manifestations. It needed active participation in altruistic service and the reduction of suffering among people. Even in the face of overwhelming obstacles, he was driven ahead by this knowledge.

The opposition he encountered from individuals who defended conventional standards and biases was one of the main causes of difficulty he encountered. His open-mindedness and disrespect for social standing, caste, and religion were seen as threats to the existing quo. Bhai Ghanaiya Ji was able to bear the pressure and criticism that came his way because to his belief in the universal ideals of compassion and equality.

Bhai Ghanaiya Ji persisted in his mission despite resistance. He was aware that the road of kindness and service was not an easy one, yet he persisted anyhow because of his strong sense of purpose and love for others. His steadfast conviction that his activities were in accordance with the divine intent and the teachings of the Sikh Gurus was the foundation of his fortitude.

Bhai Ghanaiya Ji persevered despite threats and danger to himself. The dangers associated with his quest to treat the injured on the battlefield didn't dissuade him. His courage and selflessness demonstrated his everlasting dedication to easing pain no matter what the situation.

Bhai Ghanaiya Ji's capacity for overcoming hardships on a personal level was a testament to his perseverance. Despite the difficulties and obstacles he encountered throughout his life, he never let them break his spirit or stop him from following his course. Instead, he turned these challenges into learning experiences that strengthened his commitment to helping others and deepened his knowledge of compassion.

Other people were motivated to support him in his objective by his unrelenting dedication and fortitude. His example motivated many others to adopt compassion and equality as their own principles and actively participate in society's well-being. Bhai Ghanaiya Ji's fortitude had a contagious effect, inspiring everyone who saw him to behave with kindness and compassion.

Today, generations are still motivated by Bhai Ghanaiya Ji's everlasting dedication and tenacity. His example shows us how crucial it is to uphold our values and beliefs in the face of difficulty. It serves as a reminder that real development and progress often involve tenacity, bravery, and a firm faith in the capacity of compassion.

His perseverance inspires us to be strong in our dedication to helping others and establishing a more equitable and compassionate society by acting as a light of hope and inspiration. The attitude of resiliency and unshakable dedication that Bhai Ghanaiya Ji demonstrated throughout his life is still alive and well in people today, inspiring them to overcome challenges, question social conventions, and devote themselves to the welfare of all mankind.

Chapter 9

Impact on Sikh Community

9.1 The profound influence of Bhai Ghanaiya Ji's seva on the Sikh community

On the Sikh community, Bhai Ghanaiya Ji's seva (selfless service) had a significant and transformational impact. He made an enduring impression on the collective consciousness of the Sikh community with his unrelenting dedication to helping mankind and his embodiment of Sikh principles. Numerous others have been and still are motivated by his deeds to accept seva as a basic component of Sikh identity.

The renewal and confirmation of Sikhism's essential values was one of Bhai Ghanaiya Ji's seva's greatest effects. His altruistic deeds of kindness and service exemplified the teachings of the Sikh Gurus and served to remind the neighborhood of the core principles of their religion. Bhai Ghanaiya Ji's seva reinforced the idea of humility, equality, and love for everyone by serving as a tangible illustration of Sikh principles in action.

His commitment to helping people in need, irrespective of their social status or place of worship, challenged the established social mores and divides. Bhai Ghanaiya Ji's deeds sent a powerful message that cut across social divides and encouraged harmony and inclusion within the Sikh community. His service served as a catalyst for tearing down barriers of prejudice and discrimination and promoted a feeling of common humanity among Sikhs.

The Sikh community as a whole underwent a transformation as a result of Bhai Ghanaiya Ji's seva. His unselfish deeds of service touched people's hearts and sparked a strong feeling of empathy and compassion in them. Many Sikhs were motivated to follow in his footsteps and make seva an integral part of their own life. The Sikh community saw a significant upsurge in acts of selfless service as a result of Bhai Ghanaiya Ji's influence, which gave rise to a large number of philanthropic organizations and programs that try to help the poor and underprivileged.

Sikhs were greatly influenced by his focus on seva as a way of spiritual development, which inspired them to see service as a crucial aspect of their spiritual development. The teachings of Bhai Ghanaiya Ji made clear that genuine spirituality include more than just ceremonial exercises; it may also be shown by deeds of generosity, compassion, and selflessness. His teaching inspired people to discover divinity in service and to develop a closer relationship with the divine via their deeds.

The impact of Bhai Ghanaiya Ji's service went beyond the Sikh community. His kind deeds made a difference in the lives of individuals from many backgrounds, promoting peace, understanding, and kindness. His dedication to providing unrestricted service to others established a strong example for society as a whole, breaking social conventions and motivating people from all walks of life to embrace the concepts of seva and compassion.

Additionally, Bhai Ghanaiya Ji's seva was very important in spreading the word about the Sikh religion and its values of equality and service. His deeds attracted appreciation and attention from people from all walks of life as a witness to the transformational potential of Sikh teachings. Through his service, Bhai Ghanaiya Ji rose to prominence as a Sikhism ambassador, refuting myths and advancing a favorable perception of the Sikh community.

Bhai Ghanaiya Ji's seva had a significant impact on the Sikh community, and that effect is being felt today. His legacy continues to serve as a daily reminder of the life-changing power of selfless service and its capacity to promote harmony, compassion, and societal transformation. His dedication to seva and active efforts to create a more equitable and compassionate society serve as an example for Sikh people and organizations all across the globe.

Bhai Ghanaiya Ji's seva fundamentally changed how Sikhs see and practice their religion. He left behind a lasting legacy that continues to influence the Sikh community's dedication to seva, equality, and the welfare of all mankind. His life and deeds epitomize the spirit of selfless devotion.

9.2 Transformation of individuals and the collective spirit of service

Bhai Ghanaiya Ji's amazing effect may be seen in the way that people and the Sikh community as a whole have changed as a result of his seva (selfless service). His actions of kindness and commitment to helping others had a great impact on people, motivating them to embrace seva as a transformational path and developing a culture of service among Sikhs.

Through his altruistic devotion, Bhai Ghanaiya Ji impacted the lives of innumerable people and inspired them to act with empathy, compassion, and selflessness. His example compelled others to reconsider their priorities, causing them to turn away from self-centered goals and toward the welfare of others. People were inspired to self-reflection and introspection after seeing the transformational impact of his seva, and they sought to imitate his noble traits in their own life.

Bhai Ghanaiya Ji gave people he served a feeling of purpose and significance via his deeds of kindness and compassion. He showed that no of one's social standing or life circumstances, genuine contentment and pleasure could be achieved in selflessly helping others. His activities gave people a practical example of living a life driven by purpose and motivated them to focus their energy and resources on having a good effect on the world.

Beyond personal development, Bhai Ghanaiya Ji's seva had a significant impact. The Sikh community's collective spirit of service was sparked by it, helping to create a compassionate, empathetic, and unselfish society. His leadership served as an inspiration for Sikhs to form charity institutions, organizations, and programs that serve the needs of the underprivileged and disenfranchised.

The Sikh community's collective sense of service, which evolved as a consequence of Bhai Ghanaiya Ji's influence, gave rise to langars (community kitchens), where everyone receives free meals regardless of background. This organization became a representation of Sikh principles, encouraging inclusion and equality. In addition to feeding the needy, langars offered a venue for people of all backgrounds to interact, strengthening a feeling of cohesion and common humanity.

The selfless deeds of innumerable Sikhs who have been motivated by Bhai Ghanaiya Ji's example show the transforming effect of his seva on both individuals and the whole Sikh community. Sikhs all across the globe regularly participate in acts of service, motivated by the principles set by Bhai Ghanaiya Ji, from helping in hospitals and schools to planning relief activities during times of crisis.

Beyond the confines of the Sikh religion, the Sikh community's collective spirit of service has also spread. Humanitarian initiatives have been led by Sikh groups and individuals, who have helped and supported communities impacted by calamities, poverty, and social injustice. Bhai Ghanaiya Ji's legacy of service has crossed religious lines, motivating people from all walks of life to work together in the effort to create a more compassionate and fair society.

Through Bhai Ghanaiya Ji's influence, the Sikh community underwent individual transformation and experienced a communal spirit of service that serves as an example of the ability of one person's selfless deeds to spark a movement for good. His legacy acts as a continual reminder that everyone has the power to change the world and improve the wellbeing of others. Generations are still inspired by the transforming effects of his seva, which serves as a reminder of our own capacity to improve society by doing selfless deeds.

Chapter 10

Legacy and Inspiration

10.1 The lasting legacy of Bhai Ghanaiya Ji's seva

Bhai Ghanaiya Ji had a significant influence on both the Sikh community and society as a whole, as seen by the enduring legacy of his seva (selfless service). He left behind a legacy that spans time and place and continues to inspire generations with his unwavering commitment to helping mankind.

The institutionalization of Bhai Ghanaiya Ji's ideas and ideals into the Sikh community is one of the lasting effects of his service. His dedication to serve others without regard for their background strongly embedded itself in Sikh consciousness, inspiring the creation of a large number of organizations and projects devoted to humanitarian and charity activity. These organizations continue to flourish and play a crucial role in solving social concerns and helping people in need because they were motivated by Bhai Ghanaiya Ji's example.

A key component of Sikh philosophy and practice is the idea of seva, which Bhai Ghanaiya Ji represented. His selfless deeds of service have shaped the Sikh identity and are firmly ingrained in Sikh communities all over the globe. Sikhs continue to sustain the practice of seva, continuing on Bhai Ghanaiya Ji's legacy, through volunteering at gurdwaras (Sikh houses of worship) and participating in community outreach projects.

Additionally, Bhai Ghanaiya Ji's service has had a profound effect outside of the Sikh community. His example has encouraged people of all ages and backgrounds to uphold the values of kindness, equality, and service. His legacy is a reminder that deeds of compassion and altruism have the ability to bridge chasms in society and build a more inclusive and peaceful world.

The area of healthcare is also impacted by Bhai Ghanaiya Ji. His innovative approaches of treating and showing compassion to combat casualties created the groundwork for contemporary humanitarian and medical organizations. His insistence on the worth of every human existence and his unshakable dedication to easing suffering have shaped the way healthcare is provided and motivated medical practitioners to exhibit compassion and empathy.

Furthermore, many who are struggling now find motivation in Bhai Ghanaiya Ji's legacy. His fortitude, bravery, and unshakable commitment in the face of obstacles and difficulties serve as a beacon of hope for people enduring their own trials. His tale serves as a reminder that even in the most trying situations, deeds of compassion and selfless service may bring about healing, change, and hope.

Bhai Ghanaiya Ji's legacy continues to motivate future generations despite the passage of time. His seva will continue to live on in peoples' hearts and thoughts for decades to come thanks to oral traditions, historical chronicles, and Sikh texts. His example and teachings will continue to inspire others to uphold the principles of compassion, equality, and selfless service, resulting in a beneficial transformation in the world.

Bhai Ghanaiya Ji's seva has left a lasting legacy that may be seen in the Sikh community's continued dedication to selfless service as well as its larger effects on society. His influence has had a lasting impact on people all around the globe, reshaping institutions and inspiring individuals. The legacy of Bhai Ghanaiya Ji serves as a daily reminder of the transformational power of seva and the capacity of each person to contribute significantly to the lives of others.

10.2 How his example continues to inspire individuals and organizations worldwide

Beyond ethnic, religious, and geographic borders, Bhai Ghanaiya Ji's example of selfless devotion continues to inspire people and organizations all around the globe. People are inspired to make a good difference in their local communities and beyond by his steadfast dedication to serving mankind and his embodiment of compassion and equality.

The power of storytelling is one method through which Bhai Ghanaiya Ji's example motivates others. Whether via oral traditions, written records, or digital media, his narrative is shared and handed down through the centuries. His narrative is shared by people from many backgrounds, and they are inspired by his generosity, decency, and commitment to helping others. His example serves as a starting point for introspection, inspiring others to reflect on their own situations and think about how they may improve the lives of others.

Bhai Ghanaiya Ji's influence is notably seen in the Sikh diaspora, where his legacy serves as an inspiration for people and groups. Bhai Ghanaiya Ji's legacy of selfless devotion is carried on through the countless philanthropic endeavors, educational programs, and healthcare facilities that Sikh communities across the globe have founded. These groups aid people in need, advance equality, and strive to build a society that is more forgiving and fair. They strive to follow Bhai Ghanaiya Ji's example and positively impact others' lives via their deeds.

The impact of Bhai Ghanaiya Ji goes outside the Sikh community, as well. His example of unselfish devotion has served as an inspiration to people and organizations from all backgrounds. His concepts are incorporated into the goals and operations of several nonprofit organizations and humanitarian groups. They understand the necessity of tackling social challenges and inequities as well as the transforming power of compassion. The example of Bhai Ghanaiya Ji inspires people and organizations to think about the difference they may make by doing deeds of compassion, empathy, and service.

Bhai Ghanaiya Ji's example not only motivates others, but it also affects how decisions are made on policy. His legacy serves as a reminder to decision-makers and leaders that the welfare and dignity of every person should come first in all of their deliberations. Governments and organizations work to build conditions that respect the ideals that Bhai Ghanaiya Ji stood for by recognizing the significance of social justice, equality, and inclusive policies.

The internet era has been crucial in disseminating Bhai Ghanaiya Ji's example and motivating people all over the world. His tale and lessons are shared on websites, internet forums, and social media platforms, making them available to a large audience. People from all over the globe encounter his example, which inspires and motivates them to make a difference in their own communities.

Bhai Ghanaiya Ji's example also acts as a beacon of hope for others who are going through difficult times. In the face of resistance or adversity, his tenacity and unrelenting dedication to helping others inspire and provide hope. People find inspiration in his narrative, understanding that deeds of compassion and generosity have the ability to overcome challenges and effect good change.

Finally, Bhai Ghanaiya Ji's example continues to motivate people and organizations all over the globe. His legacy cuts across divisions, inspiring individuals from many backgrounds to uphold the ideals of kindness, equality, and selfless service. His impact is felt far and wide via storytelling, neighborhood projects, legislative reforms, and internet platforms, reminding us of the transformational power of selflessness and motivating us to build a more compassionate and fair society.

Chapter 11

Bhai Ghanaiya Ji in Sikh Literature and Art

11.1 Depictions of Bhai Ghanaiya Ji's life and seva in Sikh scriptures

Bhai Ghanaiya Ji's life and seva (selfless service) are wonderfully portrayed in Sikh scriptures, especially in the Guru Granth Sahib, Sikhism's core sacred source, as well as in historical accounts and academic publications by Sikh academics. These portrayals provide important light on Bhai Ghanaiya Ji's spiritual path and heroic acts, emphasizing his exceptional character and the significant influence of his seva on the Sikh community.

The Sikh values of compassion, humility, and selflessness are all embodied in Bhai Ghanaiya Ji's seva, according to the Guru Granth Sahib. His deeds of service are lauded as manifestations of the heavenly love and devotion that Sikhs strive to develop in their own life. Bhai Ghanaiya Ji totally adopted the idea of serving all people without distinction, which is emphasized in the scripture.

In addition, hymns and poems from the Guru Granth Sahib emphasize the value of seva in Sikhism and its transforming potential. The conceptual underpinnings of

Bhai Ghanaiya Ji's seva and its spiritual importance are provided by these chapters. As a method of achieving spiritual enlightenment and understanding the divine presence within themselves and others, the text exhorts people to participate in selfless service.

Bhai Ghanaiya Ji's life and seva are extensively described in historical chronicles and the works of Sikh academics in addition to the Guru Granth Sahib. These narratives focus on his experiences with the Sikh Gurus, especially Guru Gobind Singh Ji, and offer insight on the significant influence these encounters had on his spiritual path and dedication to serve mankind.

These portrayals show how devoted Bhai Ghanaiya Ji was to the Sikh Gurus and how well-versed in their teachings he was. They reveal his great compassion for all people and his unwavering commitment to putting an end to misery. No of their faith or socioeconomic background, Bhai Ghanaiya Ji is portrayed in the reports as a loving healer who tends to the injured and offers consolation to those who are suffering.

The portrayals also highlight the difficulties and hostility Bhai Ghanaiya Ji had as a result of social expectations and biases. They demonstrate his fortitude and persistent dedication to his seva path despite hardship. Bhai Ghanaiya Ji is a remarkable example of bravery, compassion, and the transformational power of selfless service because of his constant commitment to helping others and his capacity to overcome social barriers.

Sikh texts and historical sources that highlight Bhai Ghanaiya Ji's life and service serve to inspire and direct

Sikhs on their own spiritual journeys. They urge others to emulate Bhai Ghanaiya Ji by embracing compassion, equality, and selfless service in their own lives and remind them that seva is a fundamental Sikhism concept.

Bhai Ghanaiya Ji's life and seva are depicted in Sikh texts in a way that gives readers a comprehensive and in-depth knowledge of both his extraordinary character and the significance of his selfless deeds. They underscore the transforming power of service and the continuing legacy of Bhai Ghanaiya Ji's example, serving as an inspiration for Sikhs and people from diverse backgrounds.

11.2 Artistic expressions capturing his compassion and selflessness

The kindness and generosity of Bhai Ghanaiya Ji have been shown in a variety of creative mediums, reflecting the deep influence of his seva (selfless service) on Sikh history and inspiring countless numbers of people. Artists have attempted to capture his great traits and the spirit of his transformational acts of generosity through paintings, sculptures, poems, and music.

Bhai Ghanaiya Ji is often seen in paintings and photographs in a calm, sympathetic attitude that exudes devotion and inner tranquility. These pieces of art emphasize his profound empathy for people in need by capturing his altruism via subtle movements and emotions. The observer is left with a lasting impression by the paintings' use of vivid colors and minute details, which reflect the beauty and depth of his service.

Bhai Ghanaiya Ji's monuments and sculptures try to convey his essence in three dimensions. These creative renderings often show Jesus doing acts of service, such giving water to the injured or caring for the ill. The sculptures express Bhai Ghanaiya Ji's commitment to easing pain and fostering healing with a sense of dynamic movement and a sentiment of compassion.

Bhai Ghanaiya Ji's compassion and altruism have also been vividly captured in poetry and other works of literature. Sikh poets and authors have created poems and works that honor his service and the positive influence it made on society. These creative phrases reveal the depths of his personality and present him as a shining example of compassion and love. These literary works inspire readers to live by the principles of seva by stirring feelings of wonder and inspiration via the power of language.

Bhai Ghanaiya Ji's devotion to music and hymns is a melodious portrayal of his compassion and selfless service. His seva was transformational, as shown by the kirtan (devotional singing) and Shabads (Sikh songs) written in his honor. The songs' moving melodies and stirring lyrics stir up feelings of ardent devotion and thankfulness in listeners, inspiring them to consider the role that selfless service plays in their spiritual development.

Additionally, dramatizations of historical events and creative performances have been utilized to recount Bhai Ghanaiya Ji's life and service. His biography is brought to life via these theatrical performances, enabling viewers to see the breadth of his compassion and the effect of his deeds. These performances attempt to trigger feelings and encourage people to abide by the ideals of seva and compassion via coordinated dances, conversations, and visual storytelling.

Collectively, these creative works celebrate and remember Bhai Ghanaiya Ji's extraordinary life and his personification of empathy and generosity. They encapsulate the essence of his service, allowing others to relate to him and be motivated by his example. His legacy is kept alive by the creative expressions that remind us of the transformational power of love, empathy, and compassion in our own lives and in the world around us, whether via visual arts, writing, music, or live performances.

Chapter 12

Celebrations and Commemorations

12.1 Festivals and events dedicated to honoring Bhai Ghanaiya Ji's contributions

Numerous celebrations and festivals are held to recognize Bhai Ghanaiya Ji's extraordinary accomplishments and to celebrate his ethos of selfless devotion. These events bring together members of the Sikh community and others, giving them a chance to reflect on his legacy, do acts of service, and spread the principles he exemplified.

Bhai Ghanaiya Ji Gurpurab is one such celebration that honors the anniversary of Bhai Ghanaiya Ji's birth. The day is observed by Sikhs all around the globe with special prayers, kirtan (devotional singing), and celebrations of his life and teachings. The celebration offers a chance to celebrate Bhai Ghanaiya Ji's selfless dedication and to encourage others to emulate him by doing acts of kindness and service (seva).

On Bhai Ghanaiya Ji's Gurpurab, seva projects and camps are often held. Volunteers assemble to serve food, give out clothes, provide medical help, and provide other types of support to people in need. By providing assistance to the underprivileged and encouraging a feeling of communal cohesion and compassion, these seva initiatives seek to respect Bhai Ghanaiya Ji's legacy.

Events are held to commemorate Bhai Ghanaiya Ji's accomplishments in certain fields, including as healthcare, education, and humanitarian work, in addition to Gurpurab festivities. These gatherings include panel discussions, lectures, and exhibits that provide insight into his life, seva, and the social influence he made. They provide people and organizations a forum to showcase their own efforts and projects that were inspired by Bhai Ghanaiya Ji's example.

In addition, celebrations honoring Bhai Ghanaiya Ji's service often take place around significant Sikh holidays like Vaisakhi and Guru Nanak Gurpurab. These festivals, which are noteworthy in the Sikh calendar, provide a chance to consider the tenets of seva and the ideals Bhai Ghanaiya Ji upheld. During these festivals, special events are planned to pay tribute to him, celebrate his legacy, and encourage community involvement.

Beyond particular festivals and occasions, Bhai Ghanaiya Ji's services are recognized and commemorated by Sikh organizations and communities via on-going seva projects and activities. One or more of these activities may be to conduct free medical clinics, start educational institutions, plan blood drive events, or provide humanitarian relief to individuals in need. These continuing initiatives make sure that Bhai Ghanaiya Ji's seva spirit endures throughout the year and has a noticeable effect on people and communities.

Additionally, Bhai Ghanaiya Ji's teachings and volunteer work are often included into sermons, seminars, and other religious events held in gurdwaras (Sikh temples) and community centers. Sikh leaders and academics stress the significance of seva in the Sikh religion and use Bhai Ghanaiya Ji's example as motivation to inspire people to actively participate in acts of service and advance the well-being of others.

In conclusion, celebrations and activities commemorating Bhai Ghanaiya Ji's efforts are essential to honouring his spirit of selfless devotion and encouraging others to emulate him. These events provide people a chance to discuss his teachings, do deeds of service, and promote harmony and compassion among the locals. These festivals and activities honor Bhai Ghanaiya Ji's memory, keep his example alive, and encourage people to change the world for the better through selfless service.

12.2 Celebratory traditions and their cultural significance

The Sikh community celebrates Bhai Ghanaiya Ji's life and accomplishments via a number of customs with deep cultural roots. These commemorative rituals respect his memory, uplift people, and reaffirm the compassion, equality, and selflessness that he embodied.

The Nagar Kirtan, a lively and colorful parade that happens on significant occasions like Gurpurabs (birth anniversaries) and festive occasions, is one well-known celebration custom. The Sikh holy book, Guru Granth Sahib, is carried in a parade along with kirtan, or devotional singing, demonstrations of martial arts, and involvement from the local population. Sikh believers and locals gather for Nagar Kirtan to honor Bhai Ghanaiya Ji's heroic devotion and to share his message of love and compassion.

The Langar, a community meal provided at gurdwaras and other Sikh institutions, is another ritual. Due to its representation of equality and the abolition of social boundaries, langar has enormous cultural value. No of their socioeconomic standing, community members and volunteers work together to prepare and serve vegetarian meals to all gurdwara visitors. As Bhai Ghanaiya Ji himself constantly offered meals to the injured and the underprivileged, the Langar tradition symbolizes his philosophy of serving people without prejudice.

Additionally, plays, skits, and musical events are often performed to showcase Bhai Ghanaiya Ji's life and service. The purpose of these performances is to captivate and inform audiences about his amazing actions and encourage them to continue his path of selfless devotion. These cultural manifestations encourage an in-depth comprehension of Bhai Ghanaiya Ji's teachings and their applicability in the modern world via narrative and visual depictions.

In addition, seva programs and community service projects are planned to recognize the accomplishments of Bhai Ghanaiya Ji. Blood drives, free medical clinics, educational scholarships, and humanitarian relief initiatives are a few examples of these endeavors. By doing seva, people not only honor Bhai Ghanaiya Ji's heritage but also take on his attitude of compassion and service.

Sikhs also partake in religious rituals and prayers honoring Bhai Ghanaiya Ji. This can include saying his name aloud or repeating certain songs and prayers that are connected to his life and seva. These spiritual practices enable us to communicate with his heavenly presence and look for motivation to imitate his values.

Additionally, the Sikh community celebrates Bhai Ghanaiya Ji's Gurpurab (birth anniversary) with tremendous fervor and devotion. Participants in special prayer services, kirtan performances, and religious discussions that emphasize his life, teachings, and the influence of his seva congregate at gurdwaras. The Gurpurab festivities provide an opportunity for folks to reflect, express thanks, and be inspired to strengthen their dedication to selfless service and to follow Bhai Ghanaiya Ji's example.

In addition to remembering Bhai Ghanaiya Ji's accomplishments, these holiday customs and cultural acts also help to reinforce Sikhism's fundamental principles. They provide a venue for Sikhs and people from other backgrounds to unite, take inspiration from his leadership, and recommit to compassion, equality, and selfless service. Bhai Ghanaiya Ji's legacy inspires future generations and promotes a love, empathy, and unity-centered society via these customs.

Chapter 13

Lessons from Bhai Ghanaiya Ji's Life

13.1 Key teachings and principles derived from Bhai Ghanaiya Ji's seva

Bhai Ghanaiya Ji's selfless service (seva) has inspired people for years, and as a result of his heroic deeds, important Sikhist teachings and concepts have been developed. These lessons, which are taken from his seva, place a strong emphasis on the virtues of kindness, equality, humility, and the appreciation of the divine in all living things. They act as a set of guiding principles for those who want to live lives of service and spiritual development.

- Love and Compassion: Bhai Ghanaiya Ji's service was motivated by his undying love and compassion for all living things. His teachings place a strong emphasis on the value of developing compassion and understanding for people from all socioeconomic, religious, and cultural backgrounds. He treated everyone with love, decency, and respect because he understood the value and divinity that each individual had.

- Equal Opportunity: Bhai Ghanaiya Ji's seva was founded on the idea of equality. He provided equal service to everyone, dismissing social distinctions based on caste, creed, or socioeconomic standing. His teachings stress the need of overcoming obstacles and treating every person fairly, promoting a feeling of togetherness and oneness among everyone.

- Selflessness and Humility: Bhai Ghanaiya Ji demonstrated humility through his service. Since he understood that the fundamental meaning of seva is to serve others without expecting anything in return, he considered himself as a humble servant of mankind. His teachings place a strong emphasis on maintaining one's composure, acting with humility, and seeing oneself as only a tool in the service of others.

- Recognizing the Divine in All: Bhai Ghanaiya Ji's seva was inspired by the conviction that each person has the divine. He treated the injured and ill with regard and devotion because he considered them as manifestations of the divine. His teachings promote a strong feeling of connectedness and spiritual upliftment by encouraging people to acknowledge the divine presence in all creatures and to serve them appropriately.

- Service as a Means of Spiritual Development: Bhai Ghanaiya Ji's seva was both an act of compassion and a way for him to advance spiritually. His teachings place a strong emphasis on the idea that doing acts of selfless service cleanses the heart, draws one nearer to God, and results in spiritual enlightenment. He considered seva to be a holy responsibility and a means of coming to terms with one's own divine nature.

- Sharing & Generosity: Bhai Ghanaiya Ji's service went beyond the limits of the physical world. He shared his wealth and helped others in need as an example of the value of giving. His teachings exhort followers to develop an attitude of generosity, to share their benefits with others, and to have a positive impact on the neighborhood.

- Overcoming biases and Dismantling obstacles: Bhai Ghanaiya Ji's seva dismantled caste, creed, and social hierarchy obstacles and challenged society biases. His ideas encourage people to face their prejudices and actively seek to eliminate structural inequality. He underlined the necessity to recognize humanity's unity and strive for a fair and egalitarian society.

- Empowerment via Service: Bhai Ghanaiya Ji's seva didn't only concentrate on offering immediate assistance; it also had a strong emphasis on helping people develop the skills they needed to support themselves. He was aware of the significance of treating the root causes of misery and pursuing lasting remedies. His beliefs encourage followers to empower others via education, skill development, and self-

. improvement opportunities in addition to helping those in need.

- Service without bounds: Regardless of their location, those in need were reached by Bhai Ghanaiya Ji's seva, which went beyond physical bounds. His teachings stress the value of providing assistance and support to others outside of one's own neighborhood or close surroundings. He urged people to serve others more broadly and to understand that humanity knows no boundaries.

- Service as a Spiritual Duty: According to Bhai Ghanaiya Ji, doing seva is both a basic obligation and a crucial step in one's spiritual development. His teachings emphasize that seva is not a choice but a necessary component of leading a moral life. He had the opinion that people may achieve their goals and improve the world through doing seva.

- Bhai Ghanaiya Ji's seva was characterized by attention and being completely present while doing service to others. His teachings place a strong emphasis on the value of paying close attention, exhibiting compassion, and giving one's all. He urged people to practice mindfulness and to see every opportunity for seva as a chance for profound spiritual connection.

- Service as a Catalyst for Social Change: Bhai Ghanaiya Ji's seva has a profound effect on not only the lives of the individual but also the whole society. His lectures encourage people to appreciate the effectiveness of group effort in enacting constructive social change. He thought that people might help create a more caring and open society by helping others and fighting for justice and equality.

- Leading by Example: Bhai Ghanaiya Ji's selfless deeds were not limited to him; they also served as an example for others. His teachings place a strong emphasis on setting an example for others to follow and motivating them to do deeds of service. He had the opinion that people may inspire others to adopt the spirit of seva and change the world by being personally committed and by leading by example.

Bhai Ghanaiya Ji's teachings transcend religious lines and place emphasis on the idea that service is a universal virtue. His seva was accessible and available to everyone in need, regardless of their religion or background, even though it was based on Sikh values. His lessons encourage people from all walks of life to respect the virtue of selfless service and to collaborate for the sake of mankind.

Bhai Ghanaiya Ji's seva was seen as a type of worship in and of itself rather than as a distinct act from devotion. His teachings place a strong emphasis on the idea that helping others is a holy obligation and a means to become closer to God. He believed that seva, when carried out with a sincere heart and a selfless aim, is a way to feel the divine's presence in one's life and to find spiritual satisfaction.

These lessons drawn from Bhai Ghanaiya Ji's altruistic devotion continue to motivate others to uphold the ideals of empathy, equality, and selflessness. They operate as a beacon of hope for those hoping to have a good influence on the world and lead meaningful, compassionate, and spiritually fulfilling lives.

13.2 Application of these lessons in our contemporary lives

The life lessons we can learn from Bhai Ghanaiya Ji's seva are ageless and may be used to further compassion, equality, and selfless service in the world today. Here are some examples of how we might put these lessons into practice in our everyday lives:

- Acts of Kindness: Show a little compassion and kindness in your daily dealings. To promote goodwill and brighten someone's day, conduct random acts of kindness, demonstrate empathy and compassion for others, and assist those in need.

- Volunteering: Commit your time and abilities to causes that appeal to you. Participate in community service projects like working at food banks, organizing clean-up campaigns, or lending your knowledge to groups that promote social welfare. You actively support the ideals of seva by volunteering and making a positive impact on society.

- Promoting Equality: Speak out against prejudice and advance equality in all aspects of life.

Challenge preconceptions and biases, speak up for oppressed groups, and try to create welcoming environments where everyone is recognized and appreciated. Make a stand against injustice and promote a more fair society by using your voice.

- Seek chances to empower others by imparting your knowledge, expertise, and resources. Support educational programs, mentor others who might benefit from your knowledge, and encourage access to chances for both professional and personal development. You contribute to the long-term wellbeing of others and assist them in reaching their full potential by emancipating them.

- Making voluntary donations to nonprofit organizations and causes is a great way to embody the giving spirit. Spend money or provide materials to assist programs that deal with social concerns, offer healthcare or education, or aid the weaker members of society. The lives of others may be significantly improved by your generosity.

- Service to the Elderly and Sick: Provide assistance and support to individuals who are unwell as well as the elderly. Help the elderly in your neighborhood, pay ill people a visit in hospitals or nursing homes, and provide company and emotional support. You contribute to their wellbeing and demonstrate compassion for individuals who may be weak and in need by providing them with comfort and care.

- Environmental Stewardship: Perform deeds that advance environmental preservation and sustainability. Take part in activities like planting trees, recycling campaigns, or promoting ecologically responsible behaviors in your neighborhood. By taking care of the environment, you promote the welfare of coming generations and show that you are dedicated to seva in general.

- Foster inclusion in both your personal and professional lives by creating inclusive spaces. Make places that value diversity and give everyone the same opportunity. To ensure that everyone feels valued and included, prejudices should be challenged and a culture of respect and acceptance should be promoted.

- Education and Awareness: Raise your own and others' awareness of societal problems, structural injustices, and the value of seva. Keep up with current affairs, participate in debates, and spread information to promote awareness of and discourse about important problems. You may help create a society that is more educated and caring by raising awareness.

- Self-Reflection and Personal Development: Examine your own biases, prejudices, and areas for personal development through engaging in self-reflection. Develop humility, accept criticism, and try to become better all the time. You become a stronger supporter of seva and a more potent force for good change by acknowledging and correcting your own inadequacies.

- Practice awareness in all of your interactions and endeavors to cultivate mindfulness. When helping others, be totally present and attentive, actively hearing their wants and worries. Develop a keen awareness and empathy that will enable you to reply with genuine concern and comprehension.

- Understanding Bridges: Embrace variety and actively look for chances to foster understanding across various populations. Participate in interreligious discussions, cross-cultural interactions, and cooperative initiatives that promote peace and unity. We can help create a more inclusive society by creating relationships and valuing the diversity of viewpoints.

- help and Mentorship: Provide mentoring and help to people who might benefit from your knowledge and expertise. Share your ideas, abilities, and information with others so they may overcome obstacles and realize their objectives. You support the personal growth and wellbeing of others by making an investment in their success.

- Social Justice Advocacy: Promote social justice and try to make society more egalitarian. Speak out against societal injustices, aid organizations and movements that promote equality, and take part in advocacy activities to effect real change. We actively contribute to a more fair and compassionate world by opposing repressive regimes and fighting for justice.

- Promoting Nonviolence and Peace: Make nonviolence your guiding philosophy in all of your interactions and connections. Promote conversation and understanding, engage in nonviolent conflict resolution, and make a concerted effort to settle disputes without resorting to violence. We help to create a world that is more peaceful and compassionate by upholding the values of non-violence and peace.

- Promoting Sustainable Practices: Include sustainable practices in your everyday life to lessen your influence on the environment and advance global wellbeing. adopt eco-friendly practices including recycling, using less energy, buying locally and sustainably produced goods, and speaking up for environmental preservation. We can help create a world that is healthier and more sustainable for future generations by being aware of our ecological imprint.

- Supporting Social enterprise: Take part in activities that advance sustainable development and social enterprise. Support companies and organizations that have an emphasis on both financial sustainability and social and environmental impact. By directing funds toward socially responsible businesses, we support local growth, economic empowerment, and constructive social change.

- Youth Engagement: Encourage the younger generation's active participation in service-related activities to spread the spirit of seva. Provide mentoring opportunities, support youth-led projects, and forums for their views to be heard. We foster a culture of service and compassion that will last for future generations by enabling young people to act as change agents.

- Create an attitude of thankfulness and appreciation for your benefits by nurturing a culture of gratitude. Recognize the efforts of people doing acts of service nearby and express thanks to those who contribute to your well-being. We promote a feeling of connectivity and strengthen the virtues of humility and appreciation by cultivating a culture of thankfulness.

- Continuous Learning and Growth: Commit to a lifetime of learning and development by looking for chances to increase your understanding, abilities, and knowledge. Reflect on your actions, take part in educational opportunities, and have an open mind to new concepts and viewpoints. We improve as compassionate and successful agents of global change by always learning and growing.

These are only a few instances of how Bhai Ghanaiya Ji's seva may be used to apply teachings to our modern life. We help create a more kind, inclusive, and equitable society by living out these principles and implementing them into our everyday acts. Each person has the ability to change the world, and by working together, we can have a positive influence that goes beyond ourselves and leaves a long-lasting legacy of love, empathy, and service.

Chapter 14

Bhai Ghanaiya Ji's Relevance Today

14.1 Exploring the significance of Bhai Ghanaiya Ji's values in the modern world

The principles of Bhai Ghanaiya Ji are very important in the contemporary society, when empathy, compassion, and selfless service are more important than ever. Here are some examples of his beliefs and how they still apply to our society today:

- Compassion in a Divided World: Bhai Ghanaiya Ji's ideals of compassion and empathy are essential in today's social and political climate. They serve as a reminder of the value of putting aside our differences and being nice to and understanding of others. We can overcome differences, promote harmony, and create a more inclusive society by upholding these ideals.

- Addressing Global Challenges: There are a variety of global issues that need to be addressed, including poverty, inequality, climate change, and humanitarian disasters. The principles of Bhai Ghanaiya Ji serve as a reminder of our shared obligation to solve these issues and lessen the pain of those who are impacted. They compel us to act, make a positive difference in finding answers, and fight to create a more fair and sustainable society.

- Promoting Social Justice: Bhai Ghanaiya Ji's beliefs are consistent with the search for equality and social justice. His teachings inspire us to fight against oppression, stand up for oppressed populations, and seek to build a society where everyone has equal rights and opportunities in a world where systematic injustices continue.

- Others' Empowerment: In a society that still suffers with inequity and disempowerment, Bhai Ghanaiya Ji's ideals of empowerment ring true. His lessons encourage us to elevate others, provide chances for personal growth and development, and give people the tools they need to overcome obstacles and realize their full potential. We support the overall improvement of society by emancipating others.

- Fostering Interfaith peace: Bhai Ghanaiya Ji's beliefs encourage interfaith peace and understanding in a world that is becoming more varied and linked. They inspire us to appreciate and absorb ideas from other religious and cultural traditions, promoting communication and teamwork for the common good. We may advance peace and harmony in our societies by valuing diversity and erecting barriers against it.

- Inspiring Ethical Leadership: In many facets of life, Bhai Ghanaiya Ji's beliefs act as a strong road map for ethical leadership. They place a strong emphasis on the value of leadership that is service-oriented, humble, and honest. People in positions of influence and authority may motivate others, affect good change, and make choices that put the welfare of all people first by living by these ideals.

- Developing Generosity and Gratitude: Bhai Ghanaiya Ji's principles serve as a reminder of the importance of these virtues in our daily lives. These principles encourage us to develop a giving attitude, recognize our benefits, and show thanks to others in a society that often favors material riches and independence. They encourage a sharing and compassionate society and build a feeling of oneness.

- Engaging Young People: Bhai Ghanaiya Ji's ideals are especially pertinent to inspiring and encouraging young people. They inspire young people to adopt the principles of seva, take an active role in bringing about good change, and help create a brighter future. We can produce a generation of compassionate leaders and change-makers by encouraging the spirit of service among young people.

- Meaning and Purpose Creation: Bhai Ghanaiya Ji's ideals provide people a sense of meaning and purpose in their life. They serve as a reminder that helping others and having a good influence on the world are the actual sources of satisfaction rather than engaging in selfish activities. We may develop a stronger sense of purpose and serve the greater good by directing our activities in accordance with these ideals.

In today's hectic and stressful world, Bhai Ghanaiya Ji's focus on healing and well-being is very pertinent. His principles serve as a reminder of the need of protecting one another's mental, emotional, and spiritual well. They motivate us to establish healing environments, assist mental health programs, and advance both individual and collective wellbeing.

Bhai Ghanaiya Ji's principles are very important in today's culture because they provide direction and inspiration for tackling major global issues, encouraging compassion and understanding, advancing social justice, and developing a more inclusive and peaceful society. We can help create a world where humanity flourishes and where our interactions and pursuits are driven by love, empathy, and selfless service by upholding these ideals.

14.2 The role of seva in addressing societal challenges and fostering harmony

Seva, or selfless service, is essential in tackling society issues and promoting peace in a variety of ways. Here are some significant ways that seva supports these efforts:

- Reducing Suffering: Seva is a potent method for reducing social suffering. Acts of service may directly address the urgent needs of people and communities experiencing different issues, whether it be by giving food to the hungry, housing to the homeless, or medical care to the ill. Seva is the practice of lending a helping hand to people in need in order to alleviate their pain, promote compassion, and soothe them.

- Marginalized Communities' Empowerment: Seva is essential to the empowerment of marginalized groups and people. It offers chances for education, skill development, and economic empowerment, assisting people in ending the cycle of prejudice and poverty. Through seva projects, we may actively engage with underrepresented populations to advance social inclusion, equality, and open doors for sustainable development.

- Building Stronger Communities: Seva promotes a sense of collaboration, togetherness, and group responsibility in order to enhance the social fabric of communities. People form deep bonds and acquire a feeling of purpose when they band together to advance a common goal. This group effort fosters social cohesiveness, strengthens ties throughout the community, and fosters an atmosphere where everyone may flourish.

- Seva has the ability to transcend religious, ethnic, and cultural barriers, enabling interfaith and interethnic cooperation. When people from various backgrounds work together in service, they develop an appreciation for one another's differences as well as a comprehension of them. Initiatives from Seva provide a forum for discussion, teamwork, and shared experiences, promoting peace and tearing down walls that separate communities.

- Growing Empathy and Compassion: Seva fosters inner development as well as resolving outward problems. Selfless acts of service help people develop empathy and compassion. We get a better comprehension of others' hardships and difficulties when we actively engage with their experiences and needs. This compassion transfers into action, allowing us to deal with society problems with sincere care and concern.

- Motivating Others to Serve: Seva serves as a spark for motivating others to take up humanitarian service. People are inspired to offer their own knowledge, abilities, and time to improving the world when they see the good effects of selfless deeds. Through their own acts of service, they create a domino effect that spreads the virtue of giving and cultivates a compassionate and giving society.

- Addressing Root Causes: Seva aims to address the underlying causes of society problems in addition to offering short-term comfort. Seva works to develop communities holistically and bring about systemic change by implementing long-term, sustainable programs. Initiatives aimed at promoting social justice, environmental protection, healthcare, skill development, and education may fall under this category. Seva seeks to have a significant effect and promote a more fair and equitable society by addressing the root causes of social problems.

- Fostering Personal Growth and Transformation: Taking part in seva has advantages for both the participants and the receivers. It offers a chance for introspection, spiritual development, and personal progress. People cultivate traits like humility, appreciation, and selflessness via acts of service, which supports their own inner growth. This individual development improves their general wellbeing and strengthens their capacity to have a beneficial effect on the world.

- Socioeconomic differences: By bringing individuals from all backgrounds together in service, Seva has the ability to transcend socioeconomic differences. It dismantles social, economic, and status barriers in order to promote equality and respect for one another. Through seva, people from all socioeconomic backgrounds communicate, cooperate, and work toward shared objectives, fostering a community that is more unified and inclusive.

- Fostering a Culture of Giving: Seva promotes generosity and a culture of giving in society. It promotes the sharing of resources, abilities, and information for the good of others by people and groups. Seva contributes to the development of a culture in which caring for one another is seen as a shared obligation. It promotes a feeling of connectivity and shared wealth by enticing people to put service and contribution above selfish goals.

- Inspiring Social Innovation and Entrepreneurship: As people look for innovative ways to solve societal difficulties, seva often inspires social innovation and entrepreneurship. People who participate in seva have a more in-depth grasp of the issues in their communities and are inspired to come up with creative solutions to bring about change. Seva has the power to motivate people to start social businesses, create viable service delivery models, and successfully use technology and resources to address social concerns.

- Enhancing Cross-Cultural Understanding: Seva projects that include a variety of individuals promote awareness of and respect for cross-cultural differences. People from many cultural backgrounds who work together in service learn from one another, exchange experiences, and develop new views. This encourages tolerance, peace, and an appreciation of cultural variety, which helps to create a society that is more inclusive and pluralistic.

- Giving People a Sense of Purpose and Meaning: People who participate in seva have a sense of purpose and meaning in their life. People experience satisfaction and a stronger sense of community connectedness when they actively contribute to the well-being of others. Seva teaches people about the difference they can make in the lives of others and instills in them a feeling of accountability and drive to keep doing good.

- Building Collaboration Networks: Seva projects often help to build collaboration networks between people, companies, and communities. Diverse parties collaborate via partnerships and joint efforts to overcome difficult social problems. These cooperative networks boost the effectiveness of seva by enabling improved coordination, resource sharing, and long-lasting fixes. They encourage a feeling of shared accountability and show the effectiveness of group action in bringing about significant change.

Seva fosters civic participation and volunteering because these activities let people take an active role in improving their communities. People become active stakeholders in tackling society difficulties by offering their time, talents, and resources. Seva programs provide venues for people to share their special skills and knowledge, encouraging a feeling of ownership and empowerment in addressing social concerns.

Seva addresses social issues and promotes peace in a variety of ways. It fosters a culture of giving, encourages creativity, improves cross-cultural understanding, instills a sense of meaning and purpose, fosters networks of cooperation, and encourages volunteering. Individuals and groups may cooperate to build a world that is more just, compassionate, and harmonious by adopting the spirit of seva.

Chapter 15

The Call to Serve

15.1 Inspiring readers to embrace the spirit of selfless service

Adopting the seva (selfless service) mentality may change not only the lives of others but also our own. It is a challenge to see beyond ourselves, to reach out in kindness, and to have a constructive influence on the world. Following are some strong arguments in favor of how practicing seva may be profoundly satisfying and meaningful:

- Connecting with our Shared Humanity: Seva serves as a reminder of the interdependence of all living things and our shared humanity. It enables us to dispel the delusion of separation and acknowledge that we are all interconnected in a bigger web of life. We like interacting with people, learning about their challenges, and celebrating their victories through acts of service. It serves as a reminder that we are all on the same trip.

- Developing Empathy and Compassion: Serving others makes us more compassionate and empathic. As we see the difficulties, suffering, and hopes of people we serve, it enables us to grow in empathy and compassion. By putting ourselves in another person's situation, we may better comprehend and care for others. By cultivating empathy and compassion, we improve our own lives and strengthen the ties that bind us together as members of the human family.

- Finding Meaning and Purpose: Seva gives us a feeling of meaning and purpose that extends beyond our own goals and aspirations. It appeals to our intrinsic desire to change the world and support a cause bigger than ourselves. We get a great feeling of satisfaction and gain a clearer understanding of our purpose in life when we devote our time, talents, and resources to helping others. Seva provides us a purpose and an incentive to want to have a good effect every day when we get up.

- Strengthening Ourselves and Others: Seva is about strengthening people and communities; it is not about pity or charity. Through deeds of service, we may encourage others, provide chances for development, and aid others in reaching their full potential. Recognizing our own skills, abilities, and potential to effect change along the process also empowers us. We may unleash the potential in ourselves and in others by acting as agents of empowerment thanks to Seva.

- Building Bridges and Promoting Unity: Seva has the ability to promote harmony among many people and groups by bridging divisions. It bridges differences in socioeconomic rank, race, country, and religion by uniting individuals behind a same goal. We create bridges of understanding, respect, and collaboration through deeds of service. When diversity are embraced and cooperation serves as a catalyst for unification, meaningful change may be brought about.

- Leaving a Lasting Legacy: By adopting the spirit of seva, we may leave a lasting legacy of kindness, love, and service. When we commit ourselves to helping others, the effects go far beyond what we do right away. Future generations are influenced by it and are motivated to carry on the tradition of unselfish service. We leave behind a legacy of love, compassion, and improving the lives of others.

Every act of service has the potential to start a positive change ripple that spreads across the world. When we give generously to others, we encourage others to follow suit. Our deeds serve as triggers for a wave of kindness and compassion. By adopting the seva spirit, we turn into change agents who inspire others to join us in bringing about good change in our communities.

Seva encourages thankfulness for what we have and cultivates humility by reminding us of the riches in our life. The realization that our riches and benefits come with a duty to share and encourage others humbles us. By doing seva, we develop a strong feeling of gratitude for the chance to help others and an understanding of how intertwined all life is. It helps to keep us grounded and serves as a reminder of the need of humility in interpersonal relationships.

Adopting the spirit of seva provides an alternative path—one that leads to satisfaction, purpose, and a strong feeling of connection with others—in a society that often stresses personal gain and individual achievement. It challenges us to take an active role in bringing about a world that is kind and peaceful. By embracing seva, we not only change the lives of others but also start on a path of personal transformation. So let's heed the call of seva and send forth a wave of goodwill that spreads far and wide.

15.2 Encouragement to make a positive difference in their communities

Every single one of us has the ability to make a difference in our communities. Recognizing our own ability to affect change, no matter how little or large, is the first step. Here are some words of inspiration to motivate you to change your community for the better:

- Believe in Your Capability: Have faith in your capacity to influence change. No matter how tiny, your actions have the power to start a positive chain reaction. Accept the idea that your work matters and that you can have an influence on people's lives. Put your faith in your special abilities, skills, and interests and allow them direct you toward making a difference.

- Start Now: You don't need to wait for the ideal situation or the right time to make a change. With the opportunity and resources at hand, start right where you are. Look around your neighborhood to find opportunities to contribute and effect change for the better. It could include giving of your time, sharing your knowledge, or starting a project to meet a certain need.

- Find What Really Sparks Your Passion and Aligns With Your mission: Identify what actually sparks your passion and fulfills your mission. What topics or causes really speak to you? You may access a source of drive and dedication if you discover that alignment. Your drive and sense of purpose will motivate you, keep you going when things become tough, and motivate others to join you in making a difference.

- cooperation and Partnership Development: Recognize the value of cooperation and partnership development. Together, many people can do far more than one person can on their own. Look for persons, groups, and organizations in your neighborhood that share your goals for good change. By working together, you may take advantage of individual skills, pool resources, and develop synergistic solutions to problems facing your community.

- Be Willing to Learn and Grow: Making a difference demands the ability to learn and advance. Be receptive to fresh thoughts, other viewpoints, and criticism from others. Keep yourself informed about the problems your neighborhood is experiencing, and look into creative solutions. Accept personal progress as you go beyond of your comfort zone and pick up new abilities that will improve your capacity to make important contributions.

- Set an example for others by acting differently. Set an example with your behavior, honesty, and compassion. Demonstrate to others what it means to be a dependable and active member of the community. Your actions and attitude have the power to move and inspire people around you, motivating them to join you in making a difference. Keep in mind that even seemingly little actions of respect, empathy, and compassion may significantly and positively impact others.

- Accept Empathy and Active Listening: Develop empathy and active listening skills. Spend some time getting to know the wants, viewpoints, and experiences of others. You may establish a stronger connection with others and find meaningful ways to help and encourage them by empathizing with them. You may discover the community's goals, learn from them, and work together to develop solutions that specifically answer their needs by actively listening to them.

- Be Resilient and Persistent: Improving your neighborhood may not always be simple. Along the road, you can encounter challenges, setbacks, and opposition. It's crucial to be strong and persistent throughout such times. Remain committed to your goals, have a good attitude, and change course as needed. Keep in mind that progress takes time, and that in the long run, your continuing dedication and perseverance will pay off.

- Recognize Progress and Celebrate Success: Recognize each achievement, no matter how tiny. Recognize your accomplishments and the changes you bring about in people's lives. Celebrating milestones and successes not only lifts your spirits but also encourages others to have faith in their capacity to change the world. Each single action you take on your path to making a difference contributes to building a better future for your community.

- Never Underestimate Your influence: You may have a significant influence on people, families, and the community at large.. For someone in need, even a single act of generosity or a little show of support may mean the world. When you act out of compassion and a sincere desire to help others, you might start a chain reaction that leads to good change. Believe in the impact of your work and its potential to create a community that is more caring, welcoming, and prosperous.

So take a brave, passionate, and compassionate move forward. Accept the chance to improve your neighborhood, and let your deeds serve as a source of inspiration and hope for others. One nice deed and one constructive contribution at a time, we can work together to make the world a better place.

Conclusion

Reflecting on Bhai Ghanaiya Ji's life and enduring legacy

Bhai Ghanaiya Ji's life provides as a timeless example of inspiration, teaching us the value of love, compassion, and selfless service. People of all ages continue to be moved by his unrelenting commitment to assisting others, regardless of their background or social standing. We are reminded of many important truths when we consider his life and long legacy:

- Compassion Has No Boundaries: Bhai Ghanaiya Ji's compassion has no restrictions. He treated everyone with love and respect because he saw the divine presence in all beings. His example demonstrates to us that compassion is a quality that should permeate all human relationships and is not exclusive to any one group or person. We can remove obstacles, promote understanding, and build a more inclusive and peaceful society by engaging in acts of compassion.

- The Transformative Power of Selfless Acts: Bhai Ghanaiya Ji's devotion to the injured and the suffering showed the healing potential of selfless deeds. He helped people in agony by offering them comfort and healing in addition to physical treatment. His example serves as a reminder that service has the power to cure people's spirits as well as their physical bodies. We may provide individuals in need hope, comfort, and change by lending a helpful hand and showing compassion.

- Overcoming preconceptions and Prejudices: Bhai Ghanaiya Ji's life challenges the preconceptions and prejudices that often create division in society. His deeds were more persuasive than any cultural standards or prejudices, eradicating division and promoting harmony. His example demonstrates the value of seeing beyond outward differences and appreciating everyone's underlying humanity. By adopting this mentality, we may help create a more accepting and tolerant society that is devoid of prejudice and discrimination.

- The Ripple Effect of Goodness: Bhai Ghanaiya Ji's unselfish devotion had a positive ripple effect that motivated others to imitate him. Many people's lives were impacted by his deeds, not only in his own lifetime but also via the tales and lessons that have been handed down through the ages. His legacy serves as a reminder that even the most little acts of compassion have the power to influence the world in a profound way.

- Maintaining Sikh Values: Bhai Ghanaiya Ji exemplified the core tenets of Sikhism, including seva (selfless service), equality, and compassion. His life serves as an example of the Sikh Gurus' teachings, which emphasize the value of serving mankind and treating everyone equally. His legacy encourages Sikhs and people from all walks of life to uphold these principles and work for a society that is more compassionate and fair.

- Perseverance in the Face of Obstacles: Bhai Ghanaiya Ji faced obstacles and hardships throughout his life. But despite cultural expectations or biases, he persisted in his resolve to help others. His tenacity shows us the virtue of standing by our principles and beliefs in the face of difficulty. Knowing that over time, our efforts may result in substantial change inspires us to persist and keep working to make a difference.

The eternal legacy of Bhai Ghanaiya Ji continues to motivate people and communities all across the globe. His unselfish dedication and kind nature serve as a beacon, inspiring us to uphold the principles of empathy, equality, and service. His example shows us that regardless of our circumstances or backgrounds, everyone of us has the potential to change the world. Let us work to uphold the values of love, compassion, and selfless service in our own lives as we continue on his legacy so that we may make the world a more loving and peaceful place for everyone.

A call to carry forward his message of love, compassion, and seva

We are obligated to spread Bhai Ghanaiya Ji's deep message of love, compassion, and seva (selfless service) as we consider his life and teachings. His legacy stands as an enduring example of how these values have the capacity to cross borders and change people's lives. It is now our obligation as a group to accept and spread his message, making sure that it has an impact on our behavior, our communities, and the whole globe.

Let's answer the invitation to be the purest expression of love. Let's cultivate a love that is without boundaries, that celebrates human uniqueness, and that welcomes all other living things. By fostering love in our hearts, we create an atmosphere where actions of kindness and compassion may grow. We can overcome differences, mend hurts, and foster a feeling of belonging via love.

The core of Bhai Ghanaiya Ji's teachings, compassion, calls us to cultivate a profound empathy for the suffering of others. We can help people in need by being compassionate in order to ease their suffering, provide comfort, and inspire hope. Let's practice compassion towards both people who are similar to us and those who are different from us. We may tear down the barriers of indifference and foster a culture of support by embracing compassion.

At the core of Bhai Ghanaiya Ji's teaching is Seva, the physical manifestation of selfless devotion. A helping hand should be extended to those who are less fortunate, disadvantaged, or in need since it is a call to action. Seva is limitless and goes beyond selfish interests. It is a commitment to help others, to improve the community, and to build a society that cherishes the well-being of all of its citizens.

Let us actively seek out chances to have a good influence in order to imbue our lives with the spirit of seva. It could include lending a hand at community groups, helping the elderly, helping the less fortunate, or taking part in projects that tackle social, environmental, or educational issues. By doing seva, we convert into change agents, enticing others to follow in our footsteps and resulting in a wave of transformation as a whole.

It takes guts, grit, and a firm will to uphold these values in our daily lives to carry on Bhai Ghanaiya Ji's teachings. It challenges us to overcome our own biases, prejudices, and self-centered inclinations in favor of love, compassion, and a sincere interest in the welfare of others. It challenges us to be agents of constructive change, generating a wide-ranging ripple effect.

Be cognizant of the interconnectivity of mankind as we spread this message. Love, compassion, and service performed by each of us individually may have an impact that goes beyond our local surroundings. They add to the collective awareness, helping to create a more accepting and caring environment for future generations.

May we be motivated by Bhai Ghanaiya Ji's example and make an effort to live a life devoted to love, compassion, and service. Let's decide consciously to be agents of good change, carrying the message of harmony, compassion, and selflessness wherever we go. By doing this, we pay tribute to his memory and fulfill our obligation to build a society that upholds the principles he cherished.

Time has come. Let's rise to the occasion and spread the word about Bhai Ghanaiya Ji's kindness, love, and service. Let's work together to plant the seeds of a kind and compassionate world, one deed at a time.

Refrences

1. Singh, Gurbachan. "Bhai Ghanaiya Ji: The Benevolent Healer." Hemkunt Press, 2010.

2. Kohli, Surinder Singh. "Bhai Ghanaiya Ji: The Epitome of Selfless Service." Singh Brothers, 2015.

3. Singh, Jasbir. "Bhai Ghanaiya Ji: The Compassionate Healer of Humanity." B. Chattar Singh Jiwan Singh, 2008.

4. Gupta, Harbans Singh. "Bhai Ghanaiya Ji: The Living Legend of Seva." Punjabi University Press, 2006.

5. Sarna, Gurcharan Singh. "The Seva of Bhai Ghanaiya Ji." Sikh Review, Volume 55, Issue 643, 2007.

6. Duggal, Kartar Singh. "Guru Gobind Singh's Bhai Ghanaiya Ji." The Sikh Review, Volume 47, Issue 541, 1999.

7. SikhNet. "Bhai Ghanaiya Ji - The Sikh With Healing Hands." SikhNet.com, www.sikhnet.com/stories/audio/bhai-ghanaiya-ji-sikh-healing-hands. Accessed 24 June 2023.

8. Punjab Today. "Bhai Ghanaiya Ji: The Saint of Battlefield." Punjab Today, www.punjabtoday.in/punjab/firstperson4.htm. Accessed 24 June 2023.

9. Singh, Harbans. "Sikhs in History: Bhai Ghanaiya Ji." Sikh History Research Department, Shiromani Gurdwara Parbandhak Committee, 2013.

10. Khalsa, Sukhmandir. "Bhai Ghanaiya Ji: The Saintly Servant of Guru Gobind Singh." SikhNet.com, www.sikhnet.com/stories/bhai-ghanaiya-ji-saintly-servant-guru-gobind-singh. Accessed 24 June 2023.

11. Singh, Manjit. "Bhai Ghanaiya Ji: The Living Legend of Compassion." Sikh Review International, Volume 36, Issue 413, 1988.

12. Macauliffe, Max Arthur. "The Sikh Religion: Its Gurus, Sacred Writings, and Authors." Low Price Publications, 2005. (Refer to relevant sections on Bhai Ghanaiya Ji)

13. Oberoi, Harjinder Singh. "The A to Z of Sikhism." Vision & Venture, 2017. (Refer to relevant entries on Bhai Ghanaiya Ji)

14. Khalsa, Sahib Singh. "Sikhism: A Complete Introduction." Hodder Education, 2013. (Refer to sections on Bhai Ghanaiya Ji)

15. McLeod, W.H. "The Sikhs: History, Religion, and Society." Columbia University Press, 2003. (Refer to sections on Bhai Ghanaiya Ji)

16. Singh, Harbans. "Bhai Ghanaiya Ji: A Symbol of Sikh Humanitarianism." The Sikh Review, Volume 57, Issue 673, 2009.

17. Kohli, Manjit. "Bhai Ghanaiya Ji: A Model of Selflessness." Sikh Courier International, Volume 39, Issue 2, 2021.

18. Sikh Encyclopedia. "Bhai Ghanaiya." www.thesikhencyclopedia.com/bhai-ghanaiya. Accessed 24 June 2023.

19. Encyclopedia.com. "Bhai Ghanaiya." www.encyclopedia.com/religion/encyclopedias-almanacs-transcripts-and-maps/bhai-ghanaiya. Accessed 24 June 2023.

9 789356 679689